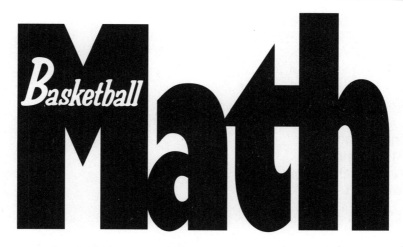

Basketball Math

SLAM-DUNK ACTIVITIES AND PROJECTS
FOR GRADES 4-8

Jack A. Coffland and David A. Coffland

GoodYearBooks

An Imprint of ScottForesman
A Division of HarperCollinsPublishers

GoodYearBooks are available for most basic curriculum subjects plus many enrichment areas. For more GoodYearBooks, contact your local bookseller or educational dealer. For a complete catalog with information about other GoodYearBooks, please write:

GoodYearBooks
ScottForesman
1900 East Lake Avenue
Glenview, IL 60025

Illustrations by Douglas Klauba.
Design by Patricia Lenihan-Barbee.

Unless otherwise acknowledged, all photographs are the property of Scott, Foresman and Company. Page abbreviations are as follows: (T) top, (C) center, (L) left, (R) right, (BG) background.
   Front cover: (L) Wide World (T) UPI/Bettman(BC) Wide
          World (R) Focus on Sports
   Back cover: (T) Wide World (B) UPI/Bettman
   Insert: Page 1 (TL) Tim Defrisco/ Allsports USA
             (TR) Steven Dunn/ Allsports USA
          · (CL) Tim Defrisco/ Allsports USA
             (CR)Tom Smart/ Allsports USA
             (BL) Steve Depaola/ Allsports USA
             (BR) Tim Defrisco/ Allsports USA
             (BG) Focus on Sports
        Page 2 (BG) Focus on Sports
        Page 3 (BG) Focus on Sports
        Page 4 (BG) Focus on Sports

Introduction for parents and teachers

When giving students in grades 4–8 problems to solve, we must be certain that they have practiced a wide variety of problems. By the time students are finished with the eighth grade, they should be proficient with problem-solving techniques involving:

- Whole Number Computation
- Fraction Computation
- Decimal Computation
- Percent Computation

One problem classification system used by many mathematicians includes both "routine" and "non-routine" problems. In other words, it is no longer appropriate to give students problems that simply review computational operations that have just been taught.

Routine problems

"Routine" problems are defined as those problems that ask students to apply a mathematical process they have learned in class in a real-life, problem-solving situation. This book defines two types of routine problems:

1. Algorithmic problems:

These are word problems (story problems) that ask children to read the problem, figure out the computational procedure required, and then apply that computational algorithm to solve the problem. For example:

Bobby scored 16 points in last night's game. Each shot he made was worth 2 points. How many baskets did he make in all?

2. Multi-step problems:

These are algorithmic problems that demand two or more computational steps in order to obtain the answer. For example:

Last year the Bruisers won three-quarters of their 12 games. This year they won 5 games. How many wins did they have over the two seasons?

Similar problems can be made with decimals or percents.

Non-routine problems

In recent years math educators have focused additional energy on "non-routine" problems—those that challenge the learner in some way. The different types of non-routine problems in this book are:

1. Challenge problems:

Problems of this type are non-routine in that the child does not know how to solve them from memory. They require the use of heuristics, the act of creating a series of steps. It is the true test of problem-solving ability. For example:

Hersey Hawkins scored 1,125 points in his senior season at Drake. He made 87 three-point shots. How many two-point shots did he make? (Hint: He scored 23 more points on free throws than he did on three-pointers.)

Challenge problems appear at the bottom of many of the activities pages.

2. Mini-project problems: Mini-project problems can often be done from one game's statistics. These projects often involve a "process"; they are not simple story problems. They are often open-ended, in that different students may obtain different answers. The process is more important than the product; the process stresses such things as multiple steps, differences in answers, and discussing your considerations to see if everyone agrees. Mini-project problems can often be formed from game statistics. An example is:

How can we interpret and understand a basketball box score? Notice that this task depends upon several variables: not every box score will be the same. Each will have different situations that must be explored. Solving mini-project problems teaches children that not all problems have simple answers, nor do all problems have one answer.

Long-term projects
Finally, since this book is meant to capture the interest of students by combining mathematics and basketball, we have suggested season-long projects. These are not really math problems; they are projects that the student can undertake that require the use of math and a knowledge of basketball. They are meant to be fun and to make math and basketball the child's hobbies.

Problems of this type are the final challenge in math. We cannot quit until we have challenged children to invent or create solutions to problems. The professional scientist, engineer, or mathematician all work to create new ideas, not simply to rehash old ideas. But the myth of mathematics learning has always been that only people in these professions must solve problems. The truth of the situation is that every day the carpenter, the clerical worker, or the grocery store clerk also invent solutions to problems.

Resources
The NCAA publishes record books each year for College athletics, listing records for the period of time that the NCAA has been the organizing association for basketball. Examples include:

Official 1994 NCAA Basketball: Records for all Divisions, Men's and Women's Basketball. NCAA, Overland Park, KS.

1992-93 National Collegiate Championships, NCAA, Overland Park, KS.

Introduction for students

This book is about basketball; it contains a great deal of interesting information about basketball—professional basketball, college men's and women's basketball, and even high school basketball. But it is also about math. It asks you to solve math problems that stem from basketball statistics, stories, and situations.

The material draws on and attempts to explain key aspects of the game of basketball. For example, you can see how defensive statistics are important. You will be given problems about defensive statistics to figure out for yourself. But you will enjoy the book much more if you also tackle the project on keeping track of defensive statistics for a game or a season. Collect all kinds of statistics on your favorite player; then see if you can figure out how he or she helps the team. Or, if you are playing basketball, keep track of your own statistics and rate yourself!

The book also contains a number of facts and figures about college and professional basketball. For example, who holds the career scoring record for women's college basketball? What college team had the best record over the past ten years? The information is presented in the form of math problems—have fun solving them or give them to your friends to solve. You will already know the answers. Enjoy!

Contents

From *BasketballMath: Slam-Dunk Activities and Projects for Grades 4–8* published by GoodYearBooks. Copyright © 1995 Jack A. Coffland and David A. Coffland.

From *BasketballMath: Slam-Dunk Activities and Projects for Grades 4–8* published by GoodYearBooks. Copyright © 1995 Jack A. Coffland and David A. Coffland.

Projects

From *BasketballMath: Slam-Dunk Activities and Projects for Grades 4–8* published by GoodYearBooks. Copyright © 1995 Jack A. Coffland and David A. Coffland.

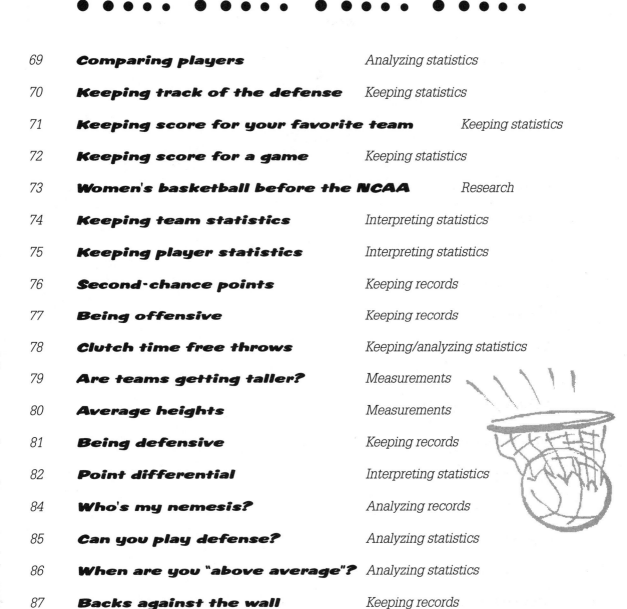

ACTIVITIES

College newspaper polls

Solve the following problems.

1. During the last week of the women's basketball season, Tennessee was the top-ranked women's team in the country. The team's record was 25 wins and 1 loss. In its last game, Tennessee beat Kentucky 95-89 in overtime. How many points were scored in the game by both teams?

   _____

2. Penn State was ranked 2nd in the women's basketball poll. The team's record was 20 wins and 1 loss. Penn State averaged 85 points a game during the regular season. How many total points did the team score in the entire season?

   _____

3. The Washington Huskies had been ranked 15th in the basketball poll, with 493 points, but they lost their last two games. Their ranking dropped to 20th, and they received only 259 points in the polls. How many fewer points did they receive in the poll after their two losses?

   _____

4. Tennessee received 874 points in the basketball poll. A total of 35 judges voted on the rankings for each team. How many points did Tennessee receive, on the average, from each judge? *(Round your answers to the nearest whole number.)*

   _____

Challenge problem

Virginia's women's team was ranked 8th in the country, with a record of 21 and 3. The number for Montana's ranking was two more than twice Virginia's number. What was Montana's ranking? *(By the way, Montana's record was 20 and 3 at the time!)*

From *Basketball Math: Slam-Dunk Activities and Projects for Grades 4–8* published by GoodYearBooks. Copyright © 1995 Jack A. Coffland and David A. Coffland.

The post-season party

Solve the following problems.

1. In the NBA play-offs, the first round is played using a "best-of-five" format. This means the team that wins three games wins the series. If there are eight first round play-off series, what is the largest number of games that can be played in the first round?

_____

2. What is the smallest number of games that can be played in the first round?

_____

3. After the first round, the play-offs are decided by "best-of-seven" series. How many games must a team win to clinch a best-of-seven series?

_____

4. There are eight teams left in the play-offs after the first round. How many series will it take to determine a champion? *(Remember, each series eliminates one team.)*

_____

5. What is the most number of games that can be played in all of the best-of-seven series?

_____

6. What is the least number of games that can be played in all of the best-of-seven series?

_____

7. Using your answers to questions 1, 2, 5, and 6, what are the most and least number of games that can be played in the NBA play-offs?

_____

March madness

Solve the following problems.

1. In the NCAA men's tournament, 64 teams participate in the first round. In this tournament, the winning team advances and the opponent is eliminated. How many games are played in the first round?

_____

2. How many games are played in the third round? How many teams participate in this round?

_____

3. How many rounds does it take to determine a champion?

_____

Challenge problem

If there are about 370 Division 1 men's basketball teams, how many rounds would have to be played in order to invite every college to the tournament?

From *Basketball Math: Slam-Dunk Activities and Projects for Grades 4–8* published by GoodYearBooks. Copyright © 1995 Jack A. Coffland and David A. Coffland.

Women's unbeaten teams

The 1986 Texas women's basketball team is the only undefeated team in NCAA women's basketball history. The team won 34 games, lost none, and won the women's basketball national championship.

1. This Texas team averaged 83.9 points per game and played 34 games. How many points did they score during the entire season? *(Reasoning question: Should this number be a whole number or a decimal?)*

_____

2. The 1986 Texas women's team had the eighth highest "scoring margin" in NCAA women's basketball history. *(The scoring margin is the difference between the winning team's score and the losing team's score.)* If the Texas women averaged 83.9 points per game, and their opponents averaged 57.2 points per game, what was the average scoring margin for Texas in 1986?

_____

3. Using the information given in problem 2, how many points were scored (on the average) during each of the Texas team's games?

_____

4. Texas made 1,162 field goals during its 34 games. How many field goals did it make, on the average, during each of those games?

_____

Men's unbeaten teams

Several men's basketball teams have enjoyed undefeated seasons, many of which resulted in a national championship. The following table shows those teams.

Team	Season	Won	Lost
North Carolina	1957	32	0
Indiana	1976	32	0
UCLA	1964	30	0
UCLA	1967	30	0
UCLA	1972	30	0
UCLA	1973	30	0
San Francisco	1956	29	0
North Carolina State	1973	27	0
Kentucky	1954	25	0
LIU-Brooklyn	1939	24	0
Seton Hall	1940	19	0
Army	1944	15	0

1. Obviously, since these teams all went undefeated, they lost no games. How many games were won by all of the teams put together?

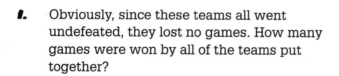

2. Some of the undefeated teams did not play in the NCAA championships. During the early years, the NCAA championship was not as popular as it is today. For example, LIU-Brooklyn went undefeated in 1939, but the Oregon Ducks won the first NCAA championship ever played during that year. How many fewer games did the Brooklyn team win in 1939 than the most recent undefeated team—the Indiana Hoosiers?

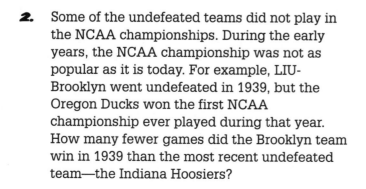

3. UCLA, during its marvelous winning streak that resulted in ten national championships, had four undefeated teams. How many wins did the Bruins have during all of those undefeated seasons put together?

_____

4. Indiana was the last undefeated men's basketball team. It achieved that honor in 1976.
   a. How many years has it been since there was an undefeated team in the NCAA?
   b. How many years have passed since the NCAA had its first undefeated team?

_____

From *Basketball Math: Slam-Dunk Activities and Projects for Grades 4–8* published by GoodYearBooks. Copyright © 1995 Jack A. Coffland and David A. Coffland.

The Warriors, state champs

In order to win the state title, the Warriors had to win four straight games at the state tournament. The scores for each game are listed in the following table.

Warriors	83	Wolverines	59
Warriors	58	Comets	52
Warriors	73	Nighthawks	45
Warriors	60	Crusaders	52

1. What was the total number of points scored by the Warriors during the tournament? What was the total for all their opponents combined?

_____

_____

2. What was the average number of points scored by the Warriors? What was the average for all their opponents combined?

_____

_____

3. What was the margin of victory for each game?

_____

_____

4. What was the average margin of victory for the Warriors during the tournament?

_____

From *Basketball Math: Slam-Dunk Activities and Projects for Grades 4–8* published by GoodYearBooks. Copyright © 1995 Jack A. Coffland and David A. Coffland.

Women's scoring champions

Solve the following problems.

1. In both 1992 and 1993 Andrea Congreaves of Mercer led NCAA women's basketball with the highest scoring average. In 1992 she scored 925 points in 28 games. What was her average score per game?

_____

2. In 1993 Andrea's scoring went down, but she still led the nation in scoring. During the 1993 season, she scored 805 points in 26 games. What was her average score per game that year?

_____

3. Despite Andrea's tremendous scoring in 1992, she does not hold the women's NCAA record for scoring. Patricia Hoskins of Mississippi Valley College earned that distinction. Patricia averaged 33.6 points per game for 27 games in 1989. How many points did she score during that year? *(Remember this is total points scored, so you have to round off your answer to a whole number.)*

_____

4. The 925 points that Andrea scored is also not the NCAA record. In 1987 Cindy Brown of Long Beach State scored 974 points in one year, averaging 27.8 points per game. How many games did Cindy Brown play in during the 1987 season?

_____

Challenge problem

Only three NCAA women players have scored 955 points or more in one season. Obviously, Cindy Brown is one. In 1993 Sheryl Swoopes of Texas Tech scored 955 points in 34 games. In 1991 Genia Miller of Cal State–Fullerton scored 969 points in 33 games. Can you estimate which player had the highest scoring average of the three players? Why or why not? Use a calculator to check the estimates.

The "Big O"

Two different basketball players have led the NCAA in scoring average for three years—Oscar Robinson of Cincinnati and Pete Maravich of Louisiana State. Both went on to have long careers in the NBA. The following chart shows Oscar Robinson's NCAA career statistics.

Oscar Robinson–6 ft., 5 in. guard

Year	Games	Field goals	Free throws	Total points	Game Average
1958	28	352	280	984	35.1
1959	30	331	316	978	32.6
1960	30	369	273	1011	33.7

1. How many field goals did Oscar Robinson make in his NCAA career?

_____

2. How many total points did Robinson score in the three seasons he played for Cincinnati? *(He ranks 7th on the all-time list of career scorers.)*

_____

3. How many free throws did Robinson make in his NCAA career?

_____

Challenge problem

Can you figure Robinson's average points over his entire NCAA career? Be careful; you can't use the game averages given in the table to calculate this. Do you know why?

"Pistol" Pete

Two different basketball players have led the NCAA in scoring average for three years—Oscar Robinson of Cincinnati and Pete Maravich of Louisiana State. Both went on to have long careers in the National Basketball Association. The following chart shows Pistol Pete Maravich's NCAA career statistics.

Year	Games	Field goals	Free throws	Total points	Game average
1968	26	432	274	1,138	43.8
1969	26	433	282	1,148	44.2
1970	31	522*	337	1,381*	44.5*

*Indicates record

2. How many total points did Pistol Pete score in the three seasons he played for LSU? *(That number ranks Maravich first in NCAA "career points"—the statistical category for total points scored in a career.)*

_____

3. How many free throws did Maravich make in his NCAA career?

_____

Challenge problem

Pistol Pete was criticized at times for shooting too much. Do you think points scored is the only statistic that is important? What other statistic might also be important when considering how many points a player scored?

1. How many field goals did Maravich make in his NCAA career?

_____

From *Basketball Math: Slam-Dunk Activities and Projects for Grades 4–8* published by GoodYearBooks. Copyright © 1995 Jack A. Coffland and David A. Coffland.

Point guards

One way to rate the effectiveness of a point guard is to calculate the assist/turnover ratio. The ratio is found by dividing the number of assists by the number of turnovers. If the point guard has a ratio larger than 1:1, then he or she is considered to be doing a good job.

Player	Assists	Turnovers	Ratio
Jason	27	12	:
Jeremy	30		2.5:1
Fred		40	1.5:1
Efrain	128	80	:

1. What is Jason's assist/turnover ratio?

_____

2. How many turnovers did Jeremy commit during the season?

_____

3. How many assists did Fred have for the season?

_____

4. What was Efrain's ratio of assists to turnovers?

_____

5. Which one of the players do you think started for the team? How did you choose your answer?

_____

Women's field goal percentage leaders

Scoring in basketball is an interesting problem. A player wants to score, but does not like to miss a shot. One interesting statistic is "field goal percentage." It expresses the percentage of shots that a player makes. Obviously, a player would like to score a lot of points and take very few shots. But some scorers take and miss a large number of shots. A player may not be helping a team if he or she misses too many shots.

The following table shows the six leading field goal percentage shooters in college women's basketball for 1993. Obviously, all six players are very good shooters; they don't miss many baskets!

Complete the table. Remember that Lidiya Varbanova, for example, could not take half a shot, so the number of field goals must come out to be a whole number. DeShawne Blocker's field goal percentage, on the other hand, should be computed to one decimal place.

Name/College	Height	Games	Field goals	Field goal attempts	Percent
Lidiya Varbanova, Boise St.	6'4"	27		294	68.0
Deneka Knowles, SE Louisiana	6'0"	26	133		65.2
DeShawne Blocker, E. Tenn St.	6'0"	25	191	294	
Cinietra Henderson, Texas	6'4"	30		325	64.9
Roschelle Vaughn, Tenn Tech	5'9"	29	272		64.6
Crystal Steward, NE Louisiana	6'2"	28	171	266	

From *Basketball Math: Slam-Dunk Activities and Projects for Grades 4–8* published by GoodYearBooks. Copyright © 1995 Jack A. Coffland and David A. Coffland.

Comparing field goal percentages

The "field goal percentage" statistic is important when you compare how making and missing a shot will help or hurt a team. Examine the following table for two women players in 1993.

Player	Field goals made	Field goals attempted	Field goal percent	3-Points made	3-Points attempted	3-Point percentage
Player A	282	670	42.1	2	9	22.2
Player B	272	421	64.6	1	4	25.0

Player A scored more points, but consider:

1. How many times did Player A shoot the ball and miss?

_____

2. If you assume a two-point field goal for each Player-A miss, how many points did she cost her team?

_____

3. How many times did Player B shoot the ball and miss?

_____

4. If you assume a two-point field goal for each Player-B miss, how many points did she cost her team?

_____

Challenge problem

Figure the total points scored by each player. Then: Player A shot the ball a total of 670 times when her team had the ball. Player B shot the ball a total of 421 times when her team had the ball. How many points were scored, on the average, for each time the player shot? *(Remember, three-pointers are included in the total number of shots taken.)*

UCLA's championships

The UCLA Bruins, under coach John Wooden, had an unbelievable string of national championships. No one has ever come close to UCLA's record. The following numbers show how fantastic the record is.

Year	Champion	Score	Second	Third	Fourth
1964	UCLA	98-83	Duke	Michigan	Kansas State
1965	UCLA	91-80	Michigan	Princeton	Wichita State
1966	UTEP	72-65	Kentucky	Duke	Utah
1967	UCLA	79-64	Dayton	Houston	N. Carolina
1968	UCLA	78-55	N. Carolina	Ohio State	Houston
1969	UCLA	92-72	Purdue	Drake	N. Carolina
1970	UCLA	80-69	Jacksonville	New Mexico State	St. Bonaventure
1971	UCLA	68-62	Villanova	Western Kentucky	Kansas
1972	UCLA	81-76	Florida State	N. Carolina	Louisville
1973	UCLA	87-66	Memphis State	Indiana	Providence
1974	N. Car. St.	76-64	Marquette	UCLA	Kansas
1975	UCLA	92-85	Kentucky	Louisville	Syracuse
1976	Indiana	86-68	Michigan	UCLA	Rutgers

1. How many years are covered in the chart above? _____

During this period of time:

2. How many first-place finishes did UCLA have? _____

3. How many third-place finishes did UCLA have? _____

4. How many times did UCLA fail to make the Final Four? _____

5. What was UCLA's average score during its championship games? _____

6. What was the second-place team's average score against UCLA? _____

7. What was UCLA's average margin of victory during its championship games? _____

From *Basketball Math: Slam-Dunk Activities and Projects for Grades 4-8* published by GoodYearBooks. Copyright © 1995 Jack A. Coffland and David A. Coffland.

Duke's championships

The only team to return to the Final Four several times in recent years has been the Duke Blue Devils. The team's record for Final Four appearances in recent years is listed below. If you compare Duke's streak to UCLA's on page 14, you will see how truly fantastic the UCLA streak was. Why? Because Duke's Coach Mike Krzyzewski, known as Coach "K," is considered to have done quite well to have made the Final Four as many times as he did. Answer the following questions to examine Duke's string of Final Four appearances.

Year	Champion	Score	Second	Third*
1986	Louisville	72-69	Duke	Kansas and Louisiana State
1987	Indiana	74-73	Syracuse	Nevada–LV and Providence
1988	Kansas	83-79	Oklahoma	Arizona and Duke
1989	Michigan	80-79	Seton Hall	Duke and Illinois
1990	Nevada–Las Vegas	103-73	Duke	Arkansas and Georgia Tech
1991	Duke	72-65	Kansas	Nevada–LV and North Carolina
1992	Duke	71-51	Michigan	Cincinnati and Indiana

Third- and fourth-place teams do not play each other

1. How many years are covered in the chart above?

_____

2. How many first-place finishes did Duke have during this time?

_____

3. How many second-place finishes did Duke have during this time?

_____

4. How many times was Duke tied for third during this period?

_____

5. How many times did Duke fail to make the Final Four during this period?

_____

6. What was Duke's average score during its championship games? (Don't forget its losses!)

_____

NCAA women's championship

The NCAA took over women's basketball in the early 1980s, holding the first women's Final Four in 1982. The record of women's college championships is shown below.

Year	Champion	Score	Second
1982	Louisiana Tech	72-62	Cheyney
1983	Southern Cal	69-67	Louisiana Tech
1984	Southern Cal	72-61	Tennessee
1985	Old Dominion	70-65	Georgia
1986	Texas	97-81	Southern Cal
1987	Tennessee	67-44	Louisiana Tech
1988	Louisiana Tech	56-54	Auburn
1989	Tennessee	76-60	Auburn
1990	Stanford	88-81	Auburn
1991	Tennessee	70-67	Virginia
1992	Stanford	78-62	Western Kentucky
1993	Texas Tech	84-82	Ohio State

1. Tennessee has three championships. Figure:
   a. its average score in those victories
   b. its opponent's average score
   c. the average margin of victory

2. Southern Cal, Stanford, and Louisiana Tech have each won two championships. For each team, figure:
   a. its average score in those victories
   b. its opponent's average score
   c. the average margin of victory

3. Auburn finished second three times in a row. That must have been difficult for the players to accept. They came so close, but they never won the championship. What was Auburn's average margin of defeat?

4. Which teams have won only one championship?

From *Basketball Math: Slam-Dunk Activities and Projects for Grades 4–8* published by GoodYearBooks. Copyright © 1995 Jack A. Coffland and David A. Coffland.

Sheryl Swoopes, 1993 MVP

During the 1993 Women's Basketball Division I Championships, Sheryl Swoopes from Texas Tech led her team to its first ever national championship. Sheryl had the kind of tournament that most people only dream about. She led all players in eight different offensive categories; she was named as the unanimous choice for the Women's Final Four Most Outstanding Player. Examine her statistics to see what kind of a tournament she had.

As you can see, Sheryl led the tournament in eight categories. She also scored 47 points in the championship game *(a championship game record)*, which Texas Tech won by a score of 84-82 over Ohio State. Obviously, Sheryl is a true champion. But to see how fantastic her tournament actually was, compute the rest of her statistics.

Games	5	Assists	11
Field goals	56*	Free throws	57*
Field goals attempted	110*	FT attempted	*
Field goal percent		FT percent	93.4%
Rebounds	48*	Total points	177*
Rebounds per game		Game average	*

1. What was Sheryl's field goal shooting percentage?

_____

2. How many free throws did Sheryl attempt? *(Remember, your answer must be rounded to a whole number; she can't shoot half a free throw.)*

_____

3. How many rebounds did Sheryl average for each game?

_____

4. How many points did Sheryl average for each game?

_____

Challenge problem
Sheryl made some three-point shots as well. How many?

_____

Hiding the three-point shots

Statistics can hide in a chart. Take a look, for example, at those in the following chart.

Selected top 10 single game scoring performances in an NCAA women's tournament game			
Player/Institution vs. Opponent/Year	FG	FT	Points
Lorri Bauman, Drake vs. Maryland, 1982	21	8	50
Sheryl Swoopes, Texas Tech vs. Ohio State, 1993	16	11	47
LaTunya Pollard, Long Beach St. vs. Howard, 1982	13	14	40
Kerry Bascom, Conn. vs. Toledo, 1991	13	8	39
Shannon Cate, Montana vs. Iowa, 1991	16	2	36
Sheryl Swoopes, Texas Tech vs. Colorado, 1993	10	15	36

What statistic is hiding here? The NCAA reports only field goals in this statistic; it does not reveal how many three-point shots the individual made. But if you compute the total points from the individual basket scores, you find that counting every field goal as a two-point basket and then adding in the free throws does not equal the total number of points. Therefore, some of the players listed above must have made three-point shots. How many? You figure it out. *(Hint: Some players did not make any.)*

Three-point baskets	
Lorri Bauman	
Sheryl Swoopes	
LaTunya Pollard	
Kerry Bascom	
Shannon Cate	
Sheryl Swoopes	

From *Basketball Math: Slam-Dunk Activities and Projects for Grades 4–8* published by GoodYearBooks. Copyright © 1995 Jack A. Coffland and David A. Coffland.

Mom's challenge problems

"Hey Karen," Mom shouted. "I've made up some brain teasers from Prescott's basketball games over the weekend. Do you want to try to solve them?"

"Sure," Karen replied. "Let's have them."

Here are the brain teasers for Karen—can you solve them?

1. Sade made the exact same number of free throws, two-point shots, and three-point shots. If she scored 30 points altogether in Friday's game, how many points did she score on three-point shots?

_____

2. Loni scored 35 points in Saturday's game. She did not make any three-point shots and she hit twice as many field goals as free throws. How many field goals and free throws did she make?

_____

3. During Friday's game, Prescott scored 10 more than twice as many points as Sade scored. How many did Prescott score?

_____

Free-throw streaks I

1. In the 1980–81 season Calvin Murphy of the Houston Rockets led the league in free-throw shooting percentage. He set an NBA record by making 206 free throws in 215 attempts during the season. What was Murphy's "made" free-throw percentage? *(Round off your answer to the nearest tenth of a percent.)*

_____

2. During the season, Murphy had a streak of 78 consecutive "made" free throws. This set the NBA record for most "made" foul shots in a row.
   (a) Not counting his streak, how many free throws did Murphy attempt?
   (b) How many of these did he make?

_____

_____

3. What would Murphy's "made" free-throw percentage have been without the streak?

_____

_____

_____

Challenge problem

During his streak, Murphy shot 100% from the charity stripe. If you average your answer from question 3 with 100%, do you come up with the same percentage as in question 1? Why or why not?

From *Basketball Math: Slam-Dunk Activities and Projects for Grades 4–8* published by GoodYearBooks. Copyright © 1995 Jack A. Coffland and David A. Coffland.

Free-throw streaks II

In 1993 two players made runs at Calvin Murphy's free throw shooting records. From February 5 to April 2, Mark Price of the Cleveland Cavaliers hit 77 straight foul shots. He went 212 for 228 during the rest of the season.

1. How many free throws did Price attempt? How many did he make?

_____

2. What was Price's free-throw shooting percentage for the season?

_____

3. While Price was shooting for Murphy's records, Michael Williams of the Minnesota Timberwolves was starting his own streak. Between March 24 and April 25, Williams was perfect from the foul line, hitting 84

consecutive shots. For the season, Williams hit 419 out of 462 free throws. What was Williams's percentage for the season?

_____

4. What was Williams's percentage without the streak?

_____

5. Did either Price or Williams break Murphy's record for highest free-throw percentage?

_____

Hot shots

Carrie and Anji are racing for the scoring title in their teams' conference. With one week to go in the season, their statistics look like this:

Player	Games	Points	Average	Games left
Carrie	18		16.0	2
Anji	19	305		1

Complete the table, then answer the following questions.

1. Who has the higher average at this point in the season?

   _____

2. Who has scored the most points so far?

   _____

3. If Carrie scores 14 points in her next game, will she be ahead of Anji's total?

   _____

4. Anji scores 20 points in the final game of her season. What will be her point average per game for the whole season?

   _____

5. How many points will Carrie need to score in her last game to win the scoring title?

   _____

From Basketball Math: Slam-Dunk Activities and Projects for Grades 4–8 published by GoodYearBooks. Copyright © 1995 Jack A. Coffland and David A. Coffland.

Shooting for the perimeter

When the painter gets ready to paint the court for a professional basketball team, he must use the diagram below to plan the job. The painter knows that he will have to put masking tape down before he paints each part of the court. He does this to prevent the workers from accidentally changing the lengths of the lines. In the following problems, assume that the painter puts tape on one side of each line.

Basketball court dimensions

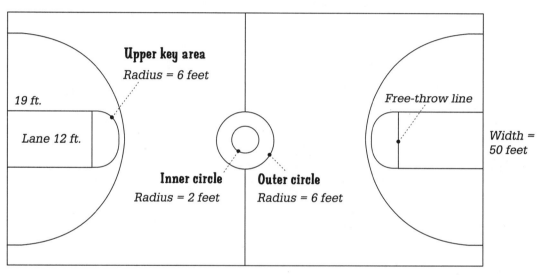

Upper key area
Radius = 6 feet

19 ft.

Lane 12 ft.

Inner circle
Radius = 2 feet

Outer circle
Radius = 6 feet

Free-throw line

Width = 50 feet

Length = 94 feet

1. How much tape will the painter need to go around the entire court?

_____

2. If the painter has already painted the perimeter of the court, he won't need to repaint the part of the lane that is on the baseline. How much tape will he need to finish both sides of the lane and the free-throw line at one end of the court?

_____

Challenge problems

What is the perimeter of the lane, including the semicircular area behind the free-throw line?

After the painter finishes painting the outer jump circle at the center of the floor, he wonders what the total length is around the edge of that circle. What is this length? *(Hint: It is called the "circumference.")*

Covering the area

After painting all of the lines on the basketball court, the painter has to paint some sections of the floor in the team colors. The areas that usually get painted are the lanes and the jump circle. (Refer to the diagram on page 23.)

1. How many square feet will be painted in the lane on each end of the court? How much area will be covered in both lanes combined? *(Note: The circular area behind the free-throw line is not part of the "lane.")*

_____

_____

2. How many square feet are painted in the jump circle *(the outer circle)* at mid-court?

_____

3. At the top of each lane, there is a half circle from which foul shots are taken. What is the area of one of these half-circles? What is the combined area of both of the half-circles?

_____

_____

4. After all of the painting is done, the painter must finish the job by applying a coat of varnish to the entire floor. What is the total area covered by the varnish?

_____

From *Basketball Math: Slam-Dunk Activities and Projects for Grades 4–8* published by GoodYearBooks. Copyright © 1995 Jack A. Coffland and David A. Coffland.

Covering the garden

In some basketball arenas, special courts or paint jobs are used to make the arena floor distinctive. The most famous of these "supreme courts" is the parquet floor at the Boston Garden in Boston, Massachusetts.

1. Suppose that the court at the Boston Garden is a standard 94-foot length by 50-foot width. If the floor extends an extra five feet at each side and three feet at each end, what are the length and width of the total floor?

_____

2. What, then, is the area of the total floor?

_____

3. If a single piece of the parquet floor is 4 feet long and 4 feet wide, what is the area of the piece?

_____

4. Use your answers to questions 2 and 3 to determine how many pieces of parquet would be needed to make the entire floor.

_____

Going the distance

Refer to the diagram on page 23 to answer the following questions

1. After making a free throw, Tracy runs back to the foul line at the other end of the court to get set to play defense. How far *(how many feet)* did she have to run to get into position?

_____

2. When Carina jumps for the opening tip in the basketball game, all of her teammates must be outside of the jump circle at mid-court. What is the closest that any of her teammates will be to the ball when it is first touched?

_____

3. Carina controls the opening tip and knocks the ball to her teammate Angela, who is standing at the top of the key. How far did the ball travel from Carina to Angela?

_____

4. In one sequence of play, Dani Jo made a free throw then ran back to the top of the key to play defense. From there she stole the ball and went straight to the basket for a lay-up. After the lay-up, the other team called for a time-out. How far did Dani Jo run between her free throw and her lay-up?

_____

Challenge problems

When does basketball/baseball player Michael Jordan have farther to run—going from baseline to baseline for a monster dunk or going from first to second on a stolen base?

_____

From *Basketball Math: Slam-Dunk Activities and Projects for Grades 4–8* published by GoodYearBooks. Copyright © 1995 Jack A. Coffland and David A. Coffland.

Shot blockers

Defensive statistics are becoming more important as people begin to understand the importance of playing strong defense. Consider the following chart showing the leading college women's shot blockers for several years.

Year	Player/Team	Games	Blocks	Average
1988	Stefanie Kasperski, Oregon	28	119	4.3
1989	Michelle Wilson, Texas South	27	151	*
1990	Simone Srubek, Fresno State	31	138	4.5
1991	Suzanne Johnson, Monmouth	23	117	5.1
1992	Denise Hogue, Charleston	28	147	5.3
1993	Chris Enger, San Diego	28		4.9

* Indicates record

1. Consider what these statistics mean to their respective teams. Most shots are blocked in close to the basket, where the shooting percentages are very high. If all of the shots that Stefanie Kasperski blocked had been good, how many more total points would Oregon's opponents have scored in each game?

_____

2. In that same manner, if all of the shots that Suzanne Johnson blocked had been good, how many more points would Monmouth's opponents have scored each game?

_____

3. Michelle Wilson holds the record for "most blocked shots per game, average." What is her record? *(Carry your answer out to one decimal point; that is the way the NCAA keeps its records.)*

_____

4. How many shots did Chris Enger block for San Diego in 1993? *(Remember, you can't block half a shot; round off your answer to the nearest whole number.)*

_____

Wanted for stealing

Another important defensive statistic is the "steal" category. A steal occurs when a defensive player on one team takes the ball before the other team can shoot. Heidi Caruso of Lafayette holds several women's records for stealing the ball from the opponent. Consider her records.

Most Steals in a Game: 14, by Heidi Caruso of Lafayette vs. Kansas State on December 5, 1992 *(tied with Natalie White of Florida A&M).*

Most Steals in a Season: Heidi Caruso, 168 steals in a 28-game season during 1993. In fact, Heidi also holds the sixth-best season record, with 144 steals in 29 games during 1992.

1. Consider what Heidi's steals meant to her team when they played Kansas State back in 1992, by answering the following questions

    a. Largest possible points prevented: Assume that Kansas State would have made three-point shots on every possession *(14)* where Heidi stole the ball. How many points did she prevent?

_____

    b. More probable: If Kansas State had made two-point shots on every possession where Heidi stole the ball, how many points did she prevent?

_____

    c. Most probable: Assume Kansas State would make half of its shots on the possessions where Heidi stole the ball. Also assume that it would have taken ten two-point shots and four three-point shots. How many points did Heidi prevent?

_____

2. Heidi made her season record of 168 steals was made in 1993. Assume the "more probable" situation *(described above)*: If her opponents had kept the ball and made half of the shots, how many points did Heidi prevent the opponents from scoring during the entire season of 1993?

_____

Challenge problem
Lafayette beat Fordham by a score of 65 to 63 during the 1993 season. Do you think Heidi had an impact on that game? Why or why not?

From *Basketball Math: Slam-Dunk Activities and Projects for Grades 4–8* published by GoodYearBooks. Copyright © 1995 Jack A. Coffland and David A. Coffland.

Home-court advantage

Atlanta won nine more home games than it lost; therefore, its record at home is +9. Atlanta's road record is -5, since the Hawks lost five more road games than they won. You can calculate these numbers by subtracting the number of games lost from the number of games won.

1992-93 season	Home			Away		
Team	W	L		W	L	
Atlanta	25	16	+9	18	23	-5
Boston	28	13		20	21	
Cleveland	29	6		19	22	
Denver	28	13		8	33	
Detroit	28	13		12	29	
Minnesota	11	30		8	33	
New York	37	4		23	18	
San Antonio	31	10		18	23	
Seattle	33	8		22	19	
Washington	15	26		7	34	

1. Complete the chart by filling in the plus or minus amount for each team's home and away records. This is the number of games that the team finished above or below .500.

_____

2. Which team had the best home record? How many games above .500 was it?

_____

3. Which team had the worst home record? How many games below .500 was its finish?

_____

4. Which team had the best road record among those listed? How far above .500 did it finish on the road?

_____

5. Which team had the worst road record for the season? How far below .500 did it fall?

_____

6. If you look closely at the chart, some of the results seem to be a little strange. Look at Denver's home and away records, for example. If you combine the two to find the team's overall record, you can see that Denver finished the season with 36 wins and 46 losses. This record did not qualify Denver for the play-offs yet its home record was much better than that of some teams that did qualify. What could be a reason for the big home court advantage?

_____

_____

_____

_____

7. In 1992–93 no NBA team had a better record on the road than it did at home; however, Charlotte had the exact same record for home and away games. If the Hornets finished the year with a total of +6, how many games above .500 were they on the road?

_____

Son of home-court advantage

Before starting this page, copy the + or − scores from page 29 onto the chart below. If you have not completed that page, do it now.

1992-93 season	Home			Away			Overall		
Team	W	L		W	L		W	L	+4
Atlanta	25	16	+9	18	23	-5	43	39	
Boston	28	13		20	21				
Cleveland	29	6		19	22				
Denver	28	13		8	33				
Detroit	28	13		12	29				
Minnesota	11	30		8	33				
New York	37	4		23	18				
San Antonio	31	10		18	23				
Seattle	33	8		22	19				
Washington	15	26		7	34				

1. The overall record of each team can be found by adding the home and away records. Calculate the overall wins and losses for each team on the chart. Atlanta's record is shown as an example.

_____

2. Atlanta was +9 at home and −5 on the road. If you add +9 and −5, you will get an answer of +4, as shown on the chart. This was the number of games above .500 for Atlanta's whole season. Use this method to fill in the last column of the chart. Check your answers against the overall record of the team.

_____

3. Which team had the best overall record? Which team had the worst?

_____

_____

4. In the same season, Utah finished +15 at home and -3 on the road. How far above or below .500 did they finish?

_____

5. New Jersey was +11 at home and -7 away for the season. Did the Nets finish with a winning or a losing record?

_____

6. How did the Orlando Magic end the season if they were +13 in Orlando and -13 everywhere else?

_____

7. The NBA regular season consists of 82 games for each team. Using this fact and the information in questions 4–6, find the final record for Utah, New Jersey, and Orlando.

_____

_____

_____

8. Which of the three teams in question 7 had the best record? What was the team's home record if it played 41 games at home?

_____

_____

From *Basketball Math: Slam-Dunk Activities and Projects for Grades 4–8* published by GoodYearBooks. Copyright © 1995 Jack A. Coffland and David A. Coffland.

Amazing championship stories

The NCAA keeps detailed records for the championship play-offs. Each year 64 teams are selected to take part in the playoffs; over the years some truly amazing things have happened, and some great basketball players have been a part of the action. Consider the following stories.

1. Christian Laettner of Duke is the coholder of the highest field goal percentage figure for one game; he shot 100%—ten shots taken, ten made—during Duke's 104-103 win over Kentucky in the regional final game in 1992. What is truly amazing was Laettner's last shot. Kentucky was ahead; Duke had time only to catch the in-bounds pass and shoot. But Laettner grabbed the pass, turned, and shot all in one motion. The shot, his tenth of the game, was perfect. Laettner scored, Kentucky lost, and Duke went on to win the national championship. What was the total number of points scored in this exciting game?

_____

2. North Carolina won the national championship in 1982, when both Michael Jordan and James Worthy played for the Tarheels. Even with these two great players, the Tarheels were locked in a tight battle with Georgetown in the championship game. It was a close contest, but with seconds left, North Carolina went ahead of Georgetown by one point, 63 to 62. Now the Tarheels had only to keep Georgetown from scoring. Georgetown brought the ball down court. The pressure was tight. The Georgetown guard turned and passed the ball backwards to a wide-open player. But it was not his teammate—it was James Worthy of North Carolina. Astonished, Worthy caught the ball and dribbled toward his basket. Time expired. North Carolina had won. Georgetown was distraught. But for one bad pass, the Hoyas might have been the national champions. How many total points were scored in this game?

_____

Three famous college shot blockers

Three very famous NBA centers hold all of the blocked shot records in the NCAA play-offs. None of the famous centers, however, could lead his team to the NCAA championship. Who are they? Read on and solve these story problems.

2. David Robinson holds the record for most blocked shots during one championship series. In 1986, his Navy team played four games before being eliminated. During those four games the "Admiral" blocked 23 shots. What was his blocked-shot average for each of the four games?

_____

3. Alonzo Mourning holds the record for most blocked shots during a career. His Georgetown team made the NCAA play-offs every year from 1989 through 1992. During that time, he played in 10 games and blocked 37 shots. If he could do this over an entire 28-game season, how many shots would "Lo" block over the season?

_____

Challenge problem

Two of these questions ask you to compute what a season's worth of shot blocks would be based upon a few games. What is wrong with using this reasoning to assume what the season record might be?

1. Shaquille O'Neal, the "Shaq," holds the NCAA championship series record for most blocked shots in one game. Louisiana State was playing Brigham Young in the first round of the 1992 play-offs. Brigham Young had several good big men, but Shaq was the master of the paint. He blocked 11 shots in one game. If Shaq could have done this every game for a 28-game season, how many shots would he have blocked over the entire season?

_____

From Basketball Math: Slam-Dunk Activities and Projects for Grades 4–8 published by GoodYearBooks. Copyright © 1995 Jack A. Coffland and David A. Coffland.

Senator Bradley's records

Some young people may not realize that Senator Bill Bradley of New Jersey was at one time a star basketball player with the Princeton Tigers and the New York Knicks. In fact, Senator Bradley still holds some NCAA play-off records. Read the following problems to learn more about these records.

1. Bill Bradley of Princeton is tied with a player from Wyoming named Fennis Dembo for having the highest free-throw percentage in one game. Both made 16 out of 16 free throws during a play-off game—Bradley against St. Joseph's in the first round of 1963 and Dembo against UCLA in the second round of 1987. How many years passed between these two record performances?

_____

2. Bradley also holds the career record for highest free-throw percentage during the NCAA play-offs. Bradley's Princeton team went to the play-offs three years in a row from 1963 through 1965. During that time, he made 87 out of 96 free-throw shots. To qualify for this record, a player must have attempted a minimum of 50 free throws. By how many attempts is Bradley over the minimum?

_____

Challenge problem

A career record like Bradley's free-throw record carries with it a minimum number of tries. Why do you think this is the case? Do you see how a record might be worthless without the minimum number of tries requirement?

The long and the short of it

In the pre-season to the 1993–94 season, the Los Angeles Lakers' roster looked like this:

Player	Height	Weight
Bowie	7'1"	263 lbs.
Campbell	6'11"	230 lbs.
Christie	6'6"	205 lbs.
Cooper	6'1"	185 lbs.
Divac	7'1"	260 lbs.
Edwards	7'1"	252 lbs.
Green	6'9"	225 lbs.
Harvey	6'11"	225 lbs.
Peeler	6'4"	212 lbs.
Smith	6'4"	205 lbs.
Threatt	6'2"	185 lbs.
Van Exel	6'1"	170 lbs.
Worthy	6'9"	225 lbs.

1. If the coach decided to put the five tallest players on the floor at once, who would they be?

_____

2. How many total inches would that team add up to?

_____

3. What would be the total height of the shortest team the coach could put on the floor?

_____

4. What is the difference in height *(in inches)* between the tallest player and the shortest player on the team? *(This number is called the "range in height.")*

_____

5. What is the average weight of the Lakers?

_____

6. What is the range of weight for the team?

_____

7. What are the total weights of the heaviest and lightest teams *(five players)* that the coach could play?

_____

8. Is the lightest team composed of the same five players as the shortest?

_____

9. The Los Angeles roster shows 13 players. The team can have only 12 active players during the season, so one player must be released. If that player is Edwards, find the new average weight of the team.

_____

Running lines

Basketball court dimensions

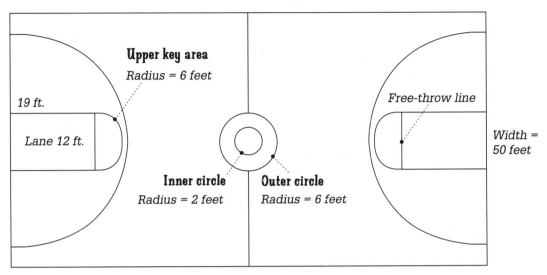

Upper key area
Radius = 6 feet

19 ft.

Lane 12 ft.

Inner circle
Radius = 2 feet

Outer circle
Radius = 6 feet

Free-throw line

*Width =
50 feet*

Length = 94 feet

1. To get into shape for the season, Heather and Stacy have to do a drill called running lines. They start at one baseline and run to the foul line and back. Then they run to the mid-court line and back. The next trip is to the far free-throw line and back. They finally are finished after they run to the far baseline and back. Their coach tells them that this is called one set of lines. How far did the girls run to complete one set of lines?

2. The team runs five complete sets of lines to start the practice. How far does each team member have to run?

3. If the team runs another five sets of lines at the end of practice, what is the total distance each player runs for the day?

Calculator problem

4. If the team keeps up this pace of running for six days a week during all 15 weeks of the season, how far will Stacy and Heather each run? How many miles is that?

The "Beast of the East"

The Big East is a fairly new college basketball conference that has been in existence only since 1980, yet its teams have won several national championships. The Big East has both a regular season champion and a post-season tournament champion.

Year	Regular Season	Conference tournament
1980	Georgetown, Syracuse, St. Johns (Tie)	Georgetown
1981	Boston College	Syracuse
1982	Villanova	Georgetown
1983	Boston Coll., Villanova, St. Johns (Tie)	St. Johns
1984	Georgetown	Georgetown
1985	St. Johns	Georgetown
1986	St. Johns, Syracuse (Tie)	St. Johns
1987	Syracuse, Georgetown, Pittsburgh	Georgetown
1988	Pittsburgh	Syracuse
1989	Georgetown	Georgetown
1990	Connecticut, Syracuse (Tie)	Connecticut
1991	Syracuse	Seton Hall
1992	Seton Hall, Georgetown, St. Johns (Tie)	Syracuse
1993	Seton Hall	Seton Hall

1. The Big East now has ten teams that play in the league. How many of those teams have won or tied for the regular season championship? How many of those teams have won the conference tournament?

_____

2. Seton Hall went several years before winning the conference tournament. Then it won two tournaments in three years. How many years was the league in existence before Seton Hall won its first tournament?

_____

3. What percentage of the teams now in the league have won or tied for the regular season championship? What percentage of the teams now in the league have won the conference tournament?

_____

From *Basketball Math: Slam-Dunk Activities and Projects for Grades 4–8* published by GoodYearBooks. Copyright © 1995 Jack A. Coffland and David A. Coffland.

Foul play I

Every coach would like his or her team not to foul at all. A personal foul can send the opponent to the free-throw line for easy points. *(Coaches call the foul line the "charity stripe" for a reason.)* If a team doesn't foul the opponent, then the opponent doesn't get the "free" points. How good or bad have players been at following the coach's instructions of "Don't Foul!"

1. In 1983 Loyola of Maryland set the women's record for most fouls in a season. The team was called for 942 personal fouls in 27 games. What was its "fouls per game" average?

    _____

2. The Boston University women's team holds the NCAA record for fewest fouls committed over a season. In 1987 the Boston U. women were called for only 261 fouls in 27 games. What was their "fouls per game" average?

    _____

3. How many more fouls did the Loyola women commit, on the average per game, than the Boston U. women?

    _____

4. Let's look at the men's figures. In 1987 the Providence College men's team was called for 966 fouls in 34 games. What was the team's average "fouls per game" average?

    _____

5. In 1962 the Air Force team was called for only 253 fouls in 23 games. What was its "fouls per game" average?

    _____

6. How many more fouls did the Providence players commit, on the average per game, than the Air Force players?

    _____

Foul play II

In high school and college basketball games, players are
disqualified (sent to the bench for the rest of the game) when
they receive their fifth foul. In the NBA, however, six fouls are
required to send a player to the bench. Consider the NBA
statistics contained in the following questions:

1. In 1976, Charlie Scott of Boston
committed 35 fouls against Phoenix in
a six-game post-season series. In how
many games did Scott foul out?

_____

2. How close *(in terms of fouls)* did
Scott come to fouling out in the next
game?

_____

3. The record for most fouls in a seven-
game series is 37. If a player commits
this many fouls, what is the smallest
possible number of times that he
could foul out?

_____

Challenge problem

The record for most fouls in a three-game
play-off series is 18. It is jointly held by
Charlie Share of St. Louis *(1956)* and Vern
Mikkelsen of Minneapolis *(1957)*. Do these
two old-time players need to worry about
losing their records? Why or why not?

From *Basketball Math: Slam-Dunk Activities and Projects for Grades 4–8* published by GoodYearBooks. Copyright © 1995 Jack A. Coffland and David A. Coffland.

Growing bigger

Today, most calculations involving big numbers are done with calculators and computers. In 1870 people may have had to add thirty big numbers by hand, but now machines do that work for us. So, here are some big number problems related to women's basketball. Get out your calculator and go to work!

Women's basketball is becoming more popular with larger crowds watching the games each year. No women play before bigger crowds than those in the Big 10 Conference. Here are some facts and figures about Big 10 women's attendance. *(Note: Paid attendance is not the same as actual attendance!)*

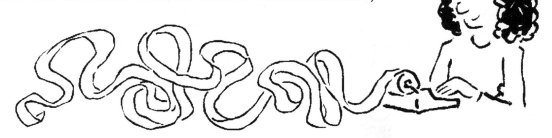

1. In 1993 the Big 10 set a national record in attendance. A total of 146 games were played; a total of 379,418 people paid to watch those games. What was the average number of paying customers attending per game?

_____

2. In 1984 a total of 118,446 people watched the Big 10 women's games; in 1993 a total of 384,962 people attended the games. How much did attendance increase between 1984 and 1993?

_____

3. In 1984 a total of 110,125 people paid to watch the Big 10 games. If 134 games were played, what was the average paid attendance per game?

_____

4. A huge increase in people watching the games occurred between the 1992 and 1993 seasons. In 1992 a total of 282,015 people paid to watch Big 10 women's basketball. This was a national record at the time. But in 1993, total paid attendance at the games jumped to 379,418, quickly establishing a new national record. What is the difference between the two records—that is, how many more people paid to attend the games in 1993 than in 1992?

_____

Tricky questions

The NCAA conferences have been changing dramatically in recent years. The results of all of these changes can be rather strange. See if you can find the answers to these "tricky" basketball questions.

1. The Big 10 Conference has been a power in basketball for many years. Such teams as Michigan *(with Glenn Rice)* and Michigan State *(with Magic Johnson)* have won the NCAA's national championship. Tricky question: How many teams are in the Big 10 Conference?

_____

2. Over the entire history of men's basketball, no league has a more glorious history than the Big 8. Kansas won a national championship in 1988; and the old Kansas teams under the famous coach Phog Allen were always national powers. Tricky question: How many teams are now in the Big 8 Conference? When did it change?

_____

_____

3. The Big East Conference is made up of eastern teams from Massachusetts, Rhode Island, Connecticut, New York, New Jersey, Pennsylvania, and Washington, DC. Yet there is one team from the Deep South in the Big East Conference. What is that team?

_____

4. The Big West Conference is made up of teams from California and Nevada. Yet, it includes two teams that are farther east than Nevada. What are these teams?

_____

_____

5. The Atlantic 10 Conference has one team from a state that does not touch the Atlantic Ocean. What is that team? Similarly, the Pacific 10 Conference has two teams from a state that does not touch the Pacific Ocean. What are those teams?

_____

_____

_____

From *Basketball Math: Slam-Dunk Activities and Projects for Grades 4–8* published by GoodYearBooks. Copyright © 1995 Jack A. Coffland and David A. Coffland.

Division by I, II, and III

One of the best things about college basketball is its popularity. Almost all colleges have a basketball team. Basketball is played at big colleges, medium-sized colleges, and very small colleges. The NCAA has three divisions, based on size, in which colleges can compete. Championships are held in Divisions I, II, and III for both men and women. Records are kept for all three divisions. Consider the following records for most points in a game by a player playing against an opponent from the same division.

Year	Division	Player	School	Points
Men				
1954	II	Clarence "Bevo" Francis	Rio Grande	113
1991	I	Kevin Bradshaw	U.S. Int.	72
1988	III	Joe DeRoche	Thomas	63
Women				
1991	II	Jacki Givens	Ft. Valley State	67
1991	III	Ann Gilbert	Oberlin	61
1987	I	Cindi Brown	Long Beach State	60

1. How many points were scored, all together, for the highest one-game men's totals? for the highest one-game women's totals? for both?

_____   _____

_____   _____

2. What is the average for the highest scores for men and women in Division I? Division II? Division III? for all three divisions combined?

_____   _____

_____   _____

3. "Bevo" Francis of Rio Grande is an interesting individual. He not only had the highest ever game score in Division II with 113 points, but he also had the second-highest game score, with 84 points, and the third-highest game score, with 82 points—all during the 1954 season. In addition, during the 1953 season, he tied for the seventh highest all-time game score with 72 points. In 1954 Francis averaged 46.5 points per game for 27 games. How many points did he score during that season?

_____

On the glass

During the play-offs, teams put extra effort into their defense. As a result, rebounding becomes very important during a play-off series. Records are kept for series that last from two to seven games.

1. The record for rebounds in a three-game play-off series is 84, held by Bill Russell of Boston. He set the record in 1957 against Syracuse. How many rebounds did Russell average per game?

_____

2. The second-best effort for rebounding in a three-game play-off is 69. Wilt Chamberlain recorded this total in 1961. How many more rebounds per game did Russell have Chamberlain?

_____

Challenge problem

Since the 1973–74 season, rebounds have been broken down into two categories: offensive and defensive. The record for offensive rebounds in a three-game series is 28, set by Moses Malone in 1982. The record for defensive rebounds is 43, set by Bob McAdoo in 1976. By comparing these records, is it possible that one of the new records would belong to Russell if offensive and defensive rebound totals had been counted in 1957? Is it possible that both records could belong to Russell?

From Basketball Math: Slam-Dunk Activities and Projects for Grades 4–8 published by GoodYearBooks. Copyright © 1995 Jack A. Coffland and David A. Coffland.

Chairman of the boards

The chart below shows rebounding records for a five-game play-off series.

	Player	Rebounds per game	Total rebounds
Total rebounds	Wilt Chamberlain–1967	32.0	
Offensive rebounds	Larry Smith–1987	7.2	
Defensive rebounds	Jack Sikma–1979	12.4	
	Karl Malone–1991	12.4	

1. Calculate the total rebounds for all four players on the chart above.

_____

2. How many defensive rebounds would Smith need to tie Chamberlain's mark?

_____

3. How many offensive rebounds would Malone need to tie Chamberlain's record for total boards?

_____

Challenge problem

During the 1978–79 season, 77% of Sikma's rebounds were on the defensive glass. If this pattern held true in the play-offs, how many offensive boards did he pull down? *(Round off your answer to the nearest whole number.)*

Where's the offense?

On November 22, 1950, the Fort Wayne Pistons played the Minneapolis Lakers. The final score was Pistons 19, Lakers 18. It was the lowest scoring game in NBA history. Fort Wayne stalled most of the game to neutralize the Laker's height advantage. The league soon introduced the 24-second shot clock, eliminating stall tactics. The 24-second rule states that a team in possession of the ball must shoot within 24 seconds, or it loses the ball.

1. The Pistons made 4 of their 13 shots from the field for a 31% average. How many points did they score from the free-throw line? *(Remember that there was no three-point shot in 1950.)*

_____

2. If the Pistons missed four foul shots, how many total free throws did they attempt as a team?

_____

3. The Lakers hit 10 of 17 from the charity stripe. How many field goals did they make?

_____

4. Laker George Mikan scored five-sixths of his team's points. With how many points did he finish the game?

_____

5. Mikan scored all of his team's field goals. He also missed as many shots as the rest of the Lakers combined. If Minneapolis attempted 18 shots, how many did Mikan miss?

_____

6. John Oldham, a guard, led the Pistons with exactly one-third of Mikan's total number of points. How many points did this "high scorer" get?

_____

7. At the end of three quarters, the score was Pistons 16, Lakers 17. How many points did each team score in the final period?

_____

8. The length of the game was 48 minutes. Did the 7,021 fans get to see an average of at least one point scored per minute?

_____

9. The lowest scoring game after the introduction of the shot clock resulted in a Boston victory over Milwaukee, 62–57. How many more points were scored in this game than in the Pistons–Lakers match-up?

_____

Where's the defense?

The highest scoring game in NBA history took place on December 13, 1983, with the Denver Nuggets hosting the Detroit Pistons. The 1983 Pistons were nothing like the 1950 Fort Wayne Pistons, scoring 186 points to the Nuggets' 184. The game took three overtime periods to complete; six players from each team scored in double figures.

1. Detroit guards Isiah Thomas and John Long led the Pistons with 47 and 41 points respectively. Did this duo score at least half of the Pistons' points?

2. Kiki Vandeweghe and Alex English led the Nuggets in scoring with 51 and 47 points, respectively. Did these two forwards account for half or more of the Denver total?

3. At the end of regulation playing time, the teams were tied at 135. How many points did Denver score in the three overtime periods? Detroit?

4. Although the teams combined for 370 points, only two three-point shots were made during the entire contest. If the teams combined for 84 points from the free-throw line, how many two-point field goals were made in the game?

5. Given that the two teams combined to make 84 free throws, and Denver made 10 more foul shots than Detroit, how many free throws did Denver convert? Detroit?

6. Including the three five-minute overtime periods, how many minutes of playing time did it take to declare a winner? *(Remember, pro games are 48 minutes long.)*

7. If the game took 3 hours and 11 minutes to complete, how much time was spent waiting for the action to resume?

8. Did the teams combine for an average of more than five points per minute?

9. On any other night, Detroit forward Kelly Tripucka's 35 points might have led the team. He scored four-fifths of his points on field goals. How many points did Tripucka have from the foul line?

From *Basketball Math: Slam-Dunk Activities and Projects for Grades 4–8* published by GoodYearBooks. Copyright © 1995 Jack A. Coffland and David A. Coffland.

Wilt's big night

On the night of March 2, 1962, the Philadelphia Warriors played the New York Knicks in Hershey, Pennsylvania. The star of the Warriors was Wilt "the Stilt" Chamberlain. Chamberlain had a reputation as a big scorer but on this night he surpassed even his own high standards. He played every minute of the Warriors' 169 to 147 victory over the Knicks; at the end of the game, he had scored exactly 100 points. Chamberlain's quarter-by-quarter scoring appears below.

Quarters	1st	2nd	3rd	4th
Points	23	18	28	31

1. How many points did Chamberlain score in the first half of the game? the second half?

_____

_____

2. What was the difference between Wilt's best and worst quarter scores?

_____

3. How many points did the rest of the Warrior team combine to score?

_____

4. Chamberlain scored 72 points from the field. How many points did he score from the free-throw line?

_____

From *Basketball Math: Slam-Dunk Activities and Projects for Grades 4–8* published by GoodYearBooks. Copyright © 1995 Jack A. Coffland and David A. Coffland.

Defending the big guy

On the night Wilt Chamberlain scored 100 points for the Philadelphia Warriors, the New York Knicks also had a big offensive night. They scored 147 points but they just couldn't stop the Warriors' big man. The Knicks box score is shown below.

Player	Field goal attempts	Field goals made	Free throw attempts	Free throws made	Points
Naulls	22	9	15	13	31
Green	7	3	0	0	6
Imhoff	7	3	1	1	7
Guerin	29	13	17	13	39
Butler	13	4	0	0	8
Buckner	26	16	1	1	33
Budd	8	6	1	1	13
Butcher	6	3	6	4	10

1. Darall Imhoff was the center for the Knicks. How many fewer points did he score than Chamberlain?

_____

2. Did the three top scorers for the Knicks—Naulls, Guerin, and Buckner—surpass Chamberlain's total?

_____

3. How many points did the Knick "B-team" score? *(The "B-team" comprises all of the players whose last name starts with the letter B.)*

_____

Double-doubles

Ethan and Angela both play basketball for the Tigers. After an away game, they compared their statistics on the bus ride home. No one had totaled up the stats, so they had to do the job themselves. Both players performed well in their games and each was interested to see if he or she earned a double-double. When a player reaches 10 in one statistic, he or she is said to have hit double figures. When a player reaches double figures in two statistical categories, he or she has scored a double-double. Ethan's stats are shown below.

Quarter	Points	Rebounds	Assists	Blocks	Steals
1	4	3	1	2	0
2	4	2	0	0	1
3	5	1	3	1	1
4	2	4	2	1	0

1. The players added up Ethan's numbers. Did Ethan reach a double-double? In which statistical categories did he do the best?

Here are Angela's stats for her game.

Quarter	Points	Rebounds	Assists	Blocks	Steals
1	2	3	1	0	5
2	3	2	4	0	3
3	1	0	4	1	0
4	0	4	2	0	3

2. After Angela added up her points, she began to think she missed a double-double. Did she reach a double-double in this game? What were her best categories?

_____

_____

Challenge problem

Try to make an educated guess about what positions Angela and Ethan play.

From *Basketball Math: Slam-Dunk Activities and Projects for Grades 4-8* published by GoodYearBooks. Copyright © 1995 Jack A. Coffland and David A. Coffland.

Triple-doubles

After their teams finished beating their arch-rivals, the two coaches called the scores and statistics in to the newspaper. Gracie had been the star of the girls' game while Cory had played well for the boys' team. The stats for each player are listed below.

Gracie

Quarter	Points	Rebounds	Assists	Blocks	Steals
1	4	5	1	1	2
2	6	4	7	2	1
3	12	3	3	4	3
4	7	4	3	0	2

Cory

Quarter	Points	Rebounds	Assists	Blocks	Steals
1	10	8	1	1	3
2	4	4	2	2	5
3	7	5	6	6	0
4	11	4	0	0	3

1. Did either player have a triple-double or a double-double? If yes, in which statistical categories did they reach double figures?

_____

_____

2. Did Gracie miss reaching double figures in a category by just one? Did she miss any categories by two?

_____

_____

3. If every assist that Gracie and Cory had led to a two-point basket, how many points did the pair create via their assists?

_____

Challenge problem

Cory had a monster scoring night in the low post. From the stats provided, can you tell if Cory had a good game defensively?

Taking attendance

During the 82-game regular season, each NBA team is seen by lots of fans. Some of these games are so important or interesting that they are moved to larger stadiums. Domed football stadiums such as the Kingdome in Seattle or the Silverdome in Detroit may be used for these "big games."

1. The biggest crowd ever to see a regular season game was the 61,983 that packed the Silverdome to watch Boston play Detroit in 1988. Average attendance in Detroit's home court is 21,454 *(in 1992–93)*. How many more fans were able to see the game held in the Silverdome?

_____

2. If the Pistons had been able to pack the Silverdome all season long, what would their home attendance have been? *(Remember, each team has 41 home games.)* Use your calculator to find the answer.

_____

3. Some teams have smaller stadiums that sell out for every game. Portland, for example, has had a streak of sellouts for some time. The Trailblazers' total attendance in the 1992–93 season was 528,408. If every game was sold out, how many fans attended each game?

_____

Challenge problem

In the 1992–93 season, 108,000 more people watched the Orlando Magic on the road than at home. Can you think of two reasons why this might be?

From *Basketball Math: Slam-Dunk Activities and Projects for Grades 4-8* published by GoodYearBooks. Copyright © 1995 Jack A. Coffland and David A. Coffland.

Keeping time

The NBA has kept track of the number of games and minutes played since 1951. Many interesting times have been recorded since then. *(Remember that a game = 48 minutes.)*

1. In the 1961–62 season, Wilt Chamberlain played 3,882 minutes in 80 games. What is unusual about this statistic?

_____

2. The record for most minutes played in one game belongs to Dale Ellis. He played 69 minutes for Seattle in 1989. What would be the smallest number of overtime periods possible in this game? *(Overtime=5 minutes.)*

_____

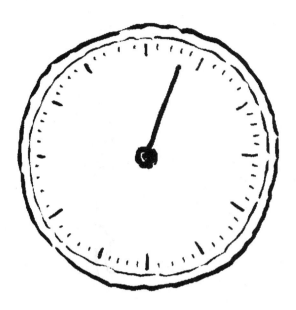

3. Kareem Abdul-Jabbar holds the record for most minutes played in a career. He played 57,446 minutes in his 20 seasons with the Milwaukee Bucs and the Los Angeles Lakers. How many days are equal to 57,446 minutes? Use your calculator to find the answer.

_____

Challenge problem

In the 1968–69 season, Walt Bellamy played for New York and Detroit. Both of these teams played a regular 82-game schedule, yet Bellamy played in 88 games. This number, 88, is still the record for most games in one season. How could Bellamy have racked up this many games?

4. Randy Smith holds the record for the most consecutive games played, with 906. Assuming there are 82 games in a season, how many seasons did this iron man play without missing a single game?

_____

NBA trivia

Sports trivia can be fun. All you have to know are a few isolated facts that not very many other people know, and you can stump all of your friends. Here are a few examples of trivia brainteasers.

1. In the 1994–95 season, Toronto will have a new NBA team, the Raptors. Is this the first Canadian team in the NBA?

_____

2. What current team traces its roots to the Rochester Royals of 1948–49?

_____

3. How many teams in the current Pacific Division (*Golden State, L.A. Clippers, L.A. Lakers, Phoenix, Portland, Sacramento, and Seattle*) have won an NBA title in their franchise history? Can you identify them?

_____

4. Which team has the record for the most wins in the regular season?

_____

5. What was the original name and location of the Washington Bullets? What was their new name the next year? What was their new name and location for the team's third season?

_____

Challenge problem

Find a basketball information book and make up trivia questions of your own.

From *Basketball Math: Slam-Dunk Activities and Projects for Grades 4–8* published by GoodYearBooks. Copyright © 1995 Jack A. Coffland and David A. Coffland.

Snack break

During the basketball season, each class in Hoopston High School sold food to raise money. The seniors sold hot dogs and pop. The juniors sold sandwiches and coffee. The sophomores brought cakes and cookies to sell. The freshmen sold candy. To save paper, the classes put all their prices on one big poster. The prices are shown below.

Hot Dogs	$1.00
Pop	.50
Sandwiches	1.75
Coffee	.50
Cakes	3.50
Cookies	.25
Candy	.50

At the end of one evening, in which both the boys' and girls' teams won big, the classes counted up their sales. The following chart shows the quantity sold of each item.

Cakes	11
Candy	48
Coffee	31
Cookies	98
Hot Dogs	76
Pop	119
Sandwiches	52

1. How much did each class make selling food at the basketball game?

_____

2. What were the total sales?

_____

The pep band blues

Solve the following problems.

1. The entire high school band cannot play at Killian High's home games. *(Two hundred fourteen musicians in a small gym would make too much noise!)* So, the pep band plays. If the pep band is made up of 27 musicians from the school band, how many school band members don't get to play at the basketball games?

_____

2. When the band members take a break, they almost always buy a drink because their lips get so dry playing all those pep songs. If all 27 band members buy a lemonade for $1.25, how much money does their refreshments cost?

_____

3. Melinda, the band property officer, has to make small copies of the music to fit on the band members' instruments. If her counter says she made 486 reduced pages of music for the band, how many music sheets do each of the 27 players get?

_____

Challenge problem

Kim, the lead trumpet player, has been in the pep band for three years. The team has 14 home games each season. If the pep band plays an average of 34 songs each night, how many songs has Kim played during her pep band career? Can you estimate how many times she has played the "Star Spangled Banner"? If so, how many?

From *Basketball Math: Slam-Dunk Activities and Projects for Grades 4–8* published by GoodYearBooks. Copyright © 1995 Jack A. Coffland and David A. Coffland.

Women's leading shooters

The following table shows the leading three-point shooters in women's college basketball.

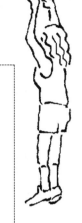

Player, Team	Last year	Years played	Games	Three-point field goals
Karen Middleton, S. Carolina	1991	4	128	317
Kathy Halligan, Creighton	1992	4	115	309
Julie Jones, Richmond	1992	4	123	309
Wendy Davis, Connecticut	1992	4	127	279
Kelly Savage, Toledo	1990	3	92	273

1. How many points did the record holder, Karen Middleton, score on three-point shots? How many points did the other players listed score on their three-point baskets?

_____

_____

2. How many three-point baskets did Karen Middleton average during each of her games?

_____

3. Are there players in the chart with more three-point baskets per game than Karen Middleton. If so, how many are there? List the players, if any, and the number of three-point baskets each averaged per game.

_____

_____

_____

_____

Challenge problems

Did you have to figure the average three-pointers per game for each of the other four players, or could you eliminate one? Why is Kathy Halligan of Creighton listed ahead of Julie Jones of Richmond in the table above?

Accuracy counts

The preceding table on three-point shots lists the total number of three-point shots made by the leading five women's basketball long-distance shooters. Interestingly, each of them also appears in the list of top 30 percentage shooters. In other words, each player made a lot of the shots that she took. Here are the actual figures for shots attempted and shots made.

Player, Team	Games	Three-point field goals	Three-pointers attempted	Percent
Karen Middleton, South Carolina	128	317	712	
Kathy Halligan, Creighton	115	309	680	
Julie Jones, Richmond	123	309	712	
Wendy Davis, Connecticut	127	279	635	
Kelly Savage, Toledo	92	273	708	

1. Before you start computing, can you predict whether Karen Middleton or Julie Jones will have the higher percentage-made figure? Why or why not?

_____

_____

2. Compute the percentage-made figures for each woman.

_____

_____

3. If the players were ranked by accuracy *(the percentage-made figure)*, what would be the new order of players?

1. _____

2. _____

3. _____

4. _____

5. _____

PROJECTS

Basketball box scores

Reading a basketball box score provides a great deal of information about the game. Look at the box score for one of the Miami Heat games, and then answer the questions that follow, using your calculator.

Player	Minutes	Field goals Made-attempted	Free throws Made-attempted	Rebounds Offense–Total	Assists	Personal fouls	Total points
Glen Rice	29	10-17	0-0	0-1	4	4	21
Grant Long	30	3-8	3-4	2-8	3	3	9
Ron Seikaly	35	8-18	3-5	7-18	4	2	19
Steve Smith	29	5-11	8-10	1-3	2	2	21
Brian Shaw	35	5-9	0-0	1-5	6	4	12
John Salley	23	5-8	4-6	4-11	1	3	14
Bimbo Coles	25	3-6	0-0	1-5	3	3	6
Willie Burton	19	5-7	2-3	0-1	0	2	12
Alec Kessler	7	2-4	0-0	0-0	0	1	5
Keith Askins	8	2-4	0-0	2-2	0	1	4

1. The third column is the field goal column. It says, for example, that Glen Rice made 10 shots and attempted 17. How many total field goals did the Heat attempt in the game?

_____

2. How many total free throws did the Heat make in this game?

_____

3. If an NBA player has six personal fouls, he has to leave the game. Which Heat player or players had the greatest number of personal fouls?

_____

4. Professional teams play 82 regular-season games. This is a busy schedule; thus coaches have to think about resting their players in each game. None of the five starters can play all 48 minutes in every game. How many total minutes did the Heat players have in this game?

_____

From *Basketball Math: Slam-Dunk Activities and Projects for Grades 4-8* published by GoodYearBooks. Copyright © 1995 Jack A. Coffland and David A. Coffland.

5. Could you have predicted the total number of minutes played in question 4 without adding up all of the minutes played by each player? *(All the information you need is there for you to get the answer with a simple multiplication problem!)*

_____

6. Ronny Seikaly had 7 offensive rebounds and 18 total rebounds. How many of his rebounds came at the defensive end of the floor? *(Hint: Subtract the offensive rebounds from the total number of rebounds, and you will find the total number of defensive rebounds.)*

_____

7. The "a" or assist statistic means that a player passed the ball to a teammate, which allowed that teammate to make a basket. How many assists did the Heat have on this night?

_____

_____

8. If the Heat starters were Glenn Rice, Grant Long, Ron Seikaly, Steve Smith, and Brian Shaw, how many points did the starting team have for the evening? How many points did the reserves score? *(These are usually described as "bench scoring" or "bench points." Teams often win games when the bench players do well.)*

_____

9. How many offensive rebounds did the Heat have on this night?

_____

From *Basketball Math: Slam-Dunk Activities and Projects for Grades 4–8* published by GoodYearBooks. Copyright © 1995 Jack A. Coffland and David A. Coffland.

Finding your team's box scores for a game

Now that you've seen what the information in the box score for a basketball game means, try doing the following:

1. Find the box score for your favorite basketball team. Can you identify what all the information means?

_____

2. Compare the box scores for a college team and a professional team. Do they provide the same information? Can you think of any information that might be found in your paper's box scores but not another's?

_____

3. Compare the winning team and the losing team. Who had more field goals? Who had more free throws? Who had more rebounds? Who had more offensive rebounds? Coaches often look at statistics such as these to help them figure out what their team is doing well—or not so well!

_____

_____

_____

4. What other interesting information about the game can you find reported in the box score?

_____

From *Basketball Math: Slam-Dunk Activities and Projects for Grades 4–8* published by GoodYearBooks. Copyright © 1995 Jack A. Coffland and David A. Coffland.

Charting shots

Coaches are concerned about where shots are taken and who takes them, so they do a shooting analysis as the game takes place. A basketball court diagram is placed on a clipboard. When a player shoots, the coach writes down the number of the player in the approximate position where the shot was taken. The coach circles the number if the shot is made. If the coach needs more room close to the basket, he or she makes other marks outside the court area, on the side where the shot was taken.

The example above covers the first half of a game played by the Townville Tigers. Assume 5 players played, numbered 1 through 5; their shot record is shown on the chart.

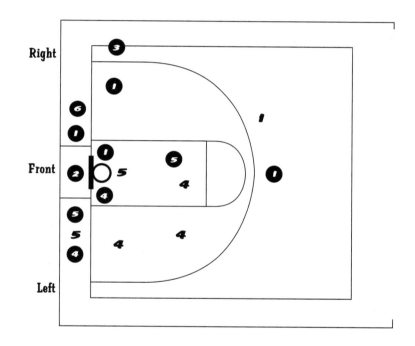

Center = number 5. This player took five shots, made three. The player made a long shot from near the free-throw line, and made two baskets close in; he or she missed two other shots close in to the basket.

Forward = number 4. This player took five shots. He or she had three misses away from the basket, and made two shots close to the left side of the basket.

Forward = number 3. This player took/made one shot— a three-pointer from the right corner.

Describe the shots for these last two players.

Guard = number 2   Guard = number 1

Constructing a shooting chart

Watch a game on TV or better yet, go to a game in person and chart the shots. A blank chart is provided below. *(Refer to the instructions on the previous page as needed.)* After you have charted all the shots in a game, summarize your chart.

1. Figure statistics:

How many shots were taken?
How many shots were made?
How many shots did each player take?
How many shots did each player make?
Calculate the shooting percentage for the team and for each player.

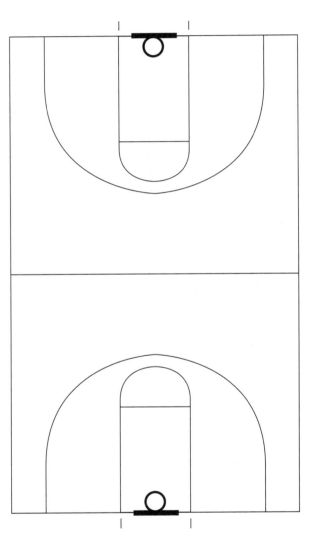

2. Examine the chart as a coach or player might examine it:

Did anyone take too many shots?
Who took shots from a place where he/she could not make them?
Who made almost all shots from a given area?
Did the team have enough "points in the paint" (meaning short, easy shots from inside the key)?
Did the team take very many three-pointers?
Who took three-point shots and made them? Missed them?

3. Make recommendations to the coach—for example:

"That forward can't make a shot more than five feet from the basket."

"That guard should not be shooting three pointshots. He missed them all."
"Pop that forward out for a long shot more often. She madethe all."

From *Basketball Math: Slam-Dunk Activities and Projects for Grades 4–8* published by GoodYearBooks. Copyright © 1995 Jack A. Coffland and David A. Coffland.

 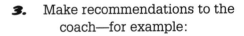

Hersey Hawkins's three-pointers

The three-point basket was introduced into NCAA play for the 1987 season. It has had a major impact on the game. No longer do teams always force the ball into the middle; no longer do defensive teams simply stand close to the basket. And no longer is a lead safe in the closing minutes. A team that is behind can score points quickly if it makes three-pointers.

In 1988 Hersey Hawkins played for Bradley. *(He has played for both Philadelphia and Charlotte in the NBA.)* Hawkins made 87 three-point baskets during that year. He scored a total of 1,125 points for the 1988 season.

Given that Hawkins scored 23 more points on free throws than he did on his three-point shots, figure the following.

1. How many field goals (two-pointers) did he make during 1988? *(Be careful; this question asks for the number of field goals, not the number of points scored on field goals.)*

_____

2. How many free throws did he make in 1988?

_____

3. Hawkins played in 31 games. What was his points-per-game average?

_____

4. Hawkins is the sixth leading scorer in the NCAA record book. He scored 3,008 points in the four years that he played college basketball. Was 1988 a better-than-average or a worse-than-average year for Hawkins? *(By the way, what was his points-per-year average over his career?)*

_____

5. Find career statistics on your favorite college or professional player. How many three-point baskets has your favorite player made in college or in the NBA?

_____

Shooting treys

The three-point play was instituted to make the game of basketball more interesting. A defensive team can choose to "clog the lane" if it wants, but if all the defensive players are standing in the lane, close to the basket, the offensive team has the opportunity to shoot easy three-point baskets.

How does your favorite team use the three-point play? Watch a game and answer the following questions.

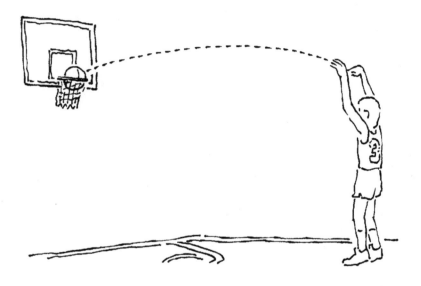

1. How many three-point shots did your favorite team attempt? How many did the other team attempt?

_____

_____

2. How many of those three-point attempts did your favorite team make? How many did the other team make?

_____

_____

3. Who scored the most points on three-point shots?

_____

4. What happens if your favorite team cannot make a three-point shot? Does it change the defense that your team faces?

_____

_____

From *Basketball Math: Slam-Dunk Activities and Projects for Grades 4–8* published by GoodYearBooks. Copyright © 1995 Jack A. Coffland and David A. Coffland.

Shooting from the charity stripe

Another vitally important statistic for a basketball team is the number of free-throw shots that it gets, and the number that it makes. To see just how important free throws really are, consider the following.

Some very good teams have lost championship games because they could not make free-throw shots. In the 1983 NCAA men's championships, for example, North Carolina State beat Houston. The University of Houston had an excellent team, including two NBA all-stars: Houston's Hakeem Olajuwon and Portland's Clyde Drexler. But North Carolina State stole the championship game from the University of Houston because, at the end of the game, Houston could not make its free-throw shots. North Carolina State deliberately fouled Houston to get the ball back, and Houston could not convert those fouls into points.

Some teams seem to get a great many foul shots. Teams that shoot jump shots from a long distance never seem to get fouled, whereas those that drive to the basket always seem to get fouled. In the 1993 NCAA men's championship game, North Carolina beat Michigan. The Michigan team actually made more baskets than North Carolina, 30 to 27. But North Carolina made 18 of 23 free throws, while Michigan made only 6 of 7 free throws.

Using this information, answer the following questions:

1. Keep track of the foul shots for your favorite team during a game. How many foul shots did it get? How many foul shots did it make? What was the percentage of "made" shots? How many foul shots did the opponent get? How many did it make? What was the percentage of "made" shots?

_____

_____

_____

_____

_____

2. You might also keep track of "crunch time" statistics. If your team was ahead with two or three minutes to play, were they fouled a lot at the end of the game? How many of those free throws did the team make?

_____

_____

3. Is there a reason why your favorite team is fouled often? Or, conversely, is there a reason why your team doesn't seem to get fouled often?

_____

_____

A new statistic

An interesting number to figure out is "average points per possession." Consider the following game statistics:

Points	90
Field goals made	28
Field goals attempted	58
Three-point goals	6
Three-point goals attempted	15
Foul shots made	16
Free throws attempted	21
Turnovers	14
Offensive rebounds	12

Now figure the team's average points per possession. First, you know the number of points scored: 90. But how many times did this team have the ball? Let's figure it out.

1. The team shot how many field goals? How many three-pointers? How many shots did the team take from the field in all?

_____

_____

2. Assume that the 12 offensive rebounds resulted in 12 extra shots. Subtract these 12 shots from your answer for question 1. This tells you how many possessions the team had that resulted in field goal attempts.

_____

3. Assume that only 3 of the free throws came after made field goals. The remaining free-throw attempts, divided by two, tells you how many possessions the team had that resulted in trips to the free-throw line.

_____

4. Find the number of turnovers the team had. (This number tells you how many times the team had the ball and did not manage to shoot.)

_____

5. Now add the answers to questions 2, 3, and 4. This tells you how many possessions the team had.

_____

6. Finally, divide the possessions into the number of points scored. The answer will tell you the average "points per possession" for this team.

_____

7. Can you calculate the number of points per possession for your favorite team for one game? for several games? How much does this statistic change when your team wins versus when it loses?

_____

_____

From Basketball Math: Slam-Dunk Activities and Projects for Grades 4–8 published by GoodYearBooks. Copyright © 1995 Jack A. Coffland and David A. Coffland.

Comparing players

Now that you know how to figure the "points per possession" statistic for a team, it might be interesting to see if individual players help or hurt their team's points per possession statistic. Let's review.

1. The points are easy to find.

2. The possessions are not. You can calculate the number of possessions by adding the number of shots taken (both regular and three-pointers), the number of turnovers, and the number of foul shots that did not come after a made basket. *(This last number can be hard to find; you may have to estimate number of possessions that ended in free throws by dividing the free-throw attempts by 2.)*

3. An individual player's points per possession, then, would be figured the same way. First, how many points did that player score? Second, how many possessions ended with this player handling the ball? You can estimate this by adding:

      a. The number of shots attempted.
      b. The number of turnovers.
      c. The number of free-throw attempts divided by 2.

Third, divide the number of possessions into the number of points scored to find the average points per possession.

4. In the paper find a box score for your favorite team. Calculate the points per possession for your team. Then, calculate the same statistic for one or more players. Did the player help the points per possession statistic by having a higher figure than the team, or did the player lower the points per possession statistic by having a lower figure than the team?

Keeping track of the defense

Watch a basketball game on television or go to a game in person.
Keep defensive statistics on your favorite team. You might want
to use the following chart. It has room for 12 players.

Player	Position	Steals	Blocks	Turnovers forced	Defensive rebounds

See if you find a pattern that allows you to
answer these questions.

1. Which position or positions is (are)
more likely to have blocked shots?

_____

2. Which position or positions is (are)
more likely to have steals?

_____

3. Who is more likely to force a
turnover?

_____

4. Who is more likely to get a defensive
rebound?

_____

From *Basketball Math: Slam-Dunk Activities and Projects for Grades 4–8* published by GoodYearBooks. Copyright © 1995 Jack A. Coffland and David A. Coffland.

Keeping score for your favorite team

Watch a basketball game on TV or go to one in person. While you watch, keep score for your favorite team. You might want to use the following chart. It has 7 categories for you to fill in.

Use tally marks in each category as you watch; summarize them when the game is over.

Number	Name	Field goals		Free throws		Rebounds		Assists	Fouls
		Made	Attempted	Made	Attempted	Off	Def		

Keeping score for a game

Of course, keeping score for one team is only half of the task. You need to keep score for both teams. Here's how you can do it.

Watch a basketball game on TV with a friend. Use two scorecards similar to the one provided on the previous page. You keep score for one team and your friend can keep score for the other team.

Summarize your results after the game to find total points scored by each player, total rebounds, and related information. Then check the paper for the next day's box score to compare your scorekeeping with the official scorekeeper's record.

Women's basketball before the NCAA

All women's basketball records included in this book come from the NCAA, the National Collegiate Athletic Association. Official NCAA women's basketball records began with the 1981–82 season, the season in which the NCAA took over women's college sports. Changes in the law that occurred about that time required that colleges spend more money on women's athletics—in an effort to make these equivalent to men's athletic programs.

This does not mean, however, that women's basketball began in 1981. Nothing could be further from the truth. An active women's basketball program existed before that time. It organized national championships and named All-American teams, among other things.

Go to the library and look up information on women's basketball prior to 1981. Read through old newspapers and magazines to see what you can find. Women's sports were not widely publicized; even so, there were some famous players, in addition to a women's professional basketball league and women's Olympic basketball championships. Your research will turn up some interesting stories about women athletes who did not get the fame or fortune they deserved.

Keeping team statistics

One of the most interesting projects you can undertake is to keep the season's statistics for your favorite team, whether that team is a high school team, a college team, or a professional team. You can get the information you need from the box scores for each game printed in your local newspaper. You can often check your statistics against the newspaper's statistics by finding out what day of each week the newspaper publishes its totals for the season to date.

What statistics should you keep? Consider the following list.

1. Scores for each game.

What was the average margin of victory for your team? (Average all your team's winning scores, average all the other teams' losing scores, and subtract to find the average difference. This is the average margin of victory.)

What was the average margin of defeat for your team?

How many more points did your team score when it won?

2. Number of field goals attempted—for both your team and the opponent.

3. Number of field goals made—for both your team and the opponent. Average these figures to find out:

Who shot more—your favorite team or the other team?

Who made more shots?

Who had the best shooting percentage?

Were these figures different in the wins and losses?

Continue by answering the four questions in problem 3 for the following categories:

4. Number of free throws attempted—for both teams.

_____   _____

_____   _____

5. Number of free throws made—for both teams.

_____   _____

_____   _____

From *Basketball Math: Slam-Dunk Activities and Projects for Grades 4–8* published by GoodYearBooks. Copyright © 1995 Jack A. Coffland and David A. Coffland.

Keeping player statistics

Another interesting season-long project is to keep statistics on your favorite player or players. Again, you can find the information you need in your daily newspaper; add up the figures to get the season-long statistics.

What statistics should you keep? Consider the following list:

1. Number of points in each game? Average to find the number of points per game. Average to find the number of points in winning and losing games. Is there a difference? Does your team win when your favorite player has a good night and lose when he or she has a bad one?

2. Number of free throws in a game? Consider the number made and the number shot. Is your favorite player a good free-throw shooter? Examine the following table to help you decide:

Making 90%—Outstanding; record performance.

Making 80% to 90%—Excellent free-throw shooter.

Making 70% to 80%—Good free-throw shooter.

Making 60% to 70%—Okay, but really not very good.

Making 60% or less: We need to work on this!!!

3. Number of field goals in a game. Again, consider the number made and the number shot. Is your favorite player an accurate shooter? Anything over 40% is okay in high school or college; professionals should do better than that. Anything over 50% is excellent for everyone. Remember that distance is often a factor; centers usually have better shooting percentages than guards.

4. Number of rebounds, steals, blocked shots, and so on. Consider your favorite player's position. If he or she is a guard, then you would expect fewer rebounds. If he or she is a center, you would expect more rebounds and blocked shots. Guards might have more steals than a center or a forward.

Second-chance points

Rebounding is one of the keys to a winning basketball team. A team that protects the defensive boards *(by rebounding most of the opponent's missed shots)* prevents that opponent from getting second and third chances to score. Similarly, a team that gets offensive rebounds *(getting the rebound after its own missed shots)* has those second and third chances to score. When watching basketball games on TV, you will often see reports on second-chance points. Second chance points are those points scored by your team *(or the opposing team)* after first missing a shot.

You can keep and interpret statistics on rebounding that will tell you about second-chance point possibilities. Consider the following:

> A team took 80 shots. The team made 40 of those shots.

1. With this information, you can figure the shooting percentage. The team shot 50%. That is excellent; you will win most games by shooting 50%.

2. Say you also know that the team collected 15 offensive rebounds. That probably means it got 15 "second-chance shots." If so, the team actually had the ball 65 times. It made a basket 40 of those times. You can figure this percentage. It's much higher than your answer to number 1, isn't it? What can we learn from this? If your team collects offensive rebounds, it will score more points.

Collect offensive rebounding statistics for your favorite team over the course of a year. You might even want to collect offensive rebounding statistics for a good team *(one with a winning record)* and a poor team *(one with a losing record.)*

There is an excellent chance that the number of offensive rebounds will be greater for the winning team. Good luck with your research.

Being offensive

It is interesting to see which players are good offensive rebounders. Some players collect large numbers of rebounds, but very few are offensive rebounds; others, such as Dennis Rodman of the San Antonio Spurs, work hard to get offensive rebounds. Let's create a "being offensive" rebounding statistic:

Consider the following situation: Sally plays for the Cougars. She gets 14 rebounds in a game. Four of these are 4 offensive rebounds. What percent of Sally's rebounds are offensive rebounds?

To answer the question, divide the number of offensive rebounds by the total number of rebounds. This gives you the "being offensive" statistic:
$$4/14 = 28\%$$

Thus, 28% of Sally's rebounds were offensive rebounds.

Using this statistic, along with the actual number of offensive rebounds can help you judge a player's ability to help his or her team with offensive rebounds.

Collect rebounding statistics for several players and then compute the "being offensive" statistic for them. Which of your players has the best percentage?

A statistic is worth more when it is collected over several games. Anyone can have a good or a bad night. But if you collect the rebounding figures for several games, you will have a statistic that gives you better information about your favorite players.

Clutch time free throws

Consider the following situation: The game is close. Your team is ahead by three points. There are only 15 seconds left. Your team has the ball. What will happen next?

Everyone knows the answer: your opponent will try to foul your worst free-throw shooter. Maybe he or she will miss; the opposing team will get the ball back, and it can try to tie the score.

It's called "clutch time." Players have to make their free throws at the end of a game, in the "clutch," to protect the lead. Are they good at it? You can figure that out.

1. Watch your favorite team on TV or go to a local game. You can find a player's free-throw shooting percentage in the paper, or they are often shown on TV as well. Once you have this number, do the following:

Wait until the last three minutes of a game. Then record:

The number of foul shots each player gets.

Whether it is a "one and one" or not.

How many shots each player makes.

Then, figure out the free-throw percentage for "clutch time."

2. Which players shot better (than their regular free-throw percentage) at the end of the game? Which ones shot worse? Repeat this process for several games. What did you find?

3. Pretend you are the coach. If you were protecting a small lead, which players would you want in the game during the last few minutes?

From *Basketball Math: Slam-Dunk Activities and Projects for Grades 4–8* published by GoodYearBooks. Copyright © 1995 Jack A. Coffland and David A. Coffland.

Are teams getting taller?

As women's basketball becomes more popular, coaches are finding and training taller women to be basketball players. Many women's basketball teams now have players that are 6 feet 2 inches tall or taller. At one time UCLA's men's basketball team, the men's national champions, played a 6-foot-1-inch forward. Today, you would never see a forward that "short" on a men's team, and you would find that most women's teams have players taller than that starting at forward and center.

How tall are the women's teams getting to be? Why don't you start a season-long project to find out?

1. Check to see when women's basketball games are broadcast in your area. Look for a local sports network on cable *(Pacific Northwest Sports, Sunshine Network, etc.)*. Or, look in your TV guide for any national or regional games that might be on one of the major networks. Or, finally, see if you can find local broadcasts of your area's college teams.

2. Watch the first five minutes of the program, when the sportscasters announce the starting lineups. Usually, at that time the player's vital statistics *(height, position, scoring average, etc.)* are also given.

3. Keep a journal in which you record the tallest players for each team. See how many women's players you can find who are 6 feet 2 inches or taller. After you are done collecting data, you might transfer all the heights to inches and graph the tallest players by team. You might even compare the graphs from one season to the next. Are teams getting taller?

From *Basketball Math: Slam-Dunk Activities and Projects for Grades 4–8* published by GoodYearBooks. Copyright © 1995 Jack A. Coffland and David A. Coffland.

Average heights

Basketball players come in all sizes. In the NBA Mugsy Boges of the Charlotte Hornets is only 5 feet 3 inches tall. By contrast, Shawn Bradley of the Philadelphia 76ers is 7 feet 6 inches tall. That is a difference of 2 feet 3 inches. There have even been NBA players who were taller than 7 feet 6 inches.

We often talk about how the "average height" of the players is getting taller. What does "average height" mean? If you add all the players' heights together, and divide by the number of players, you get the average height for a team. At one time, only 25 years ago, teams might have an average size of only 6 feet 3 inches. Now, most professional teams are much larger than that, most college teams are much larger, and even many high school teams have a much larger starting lineup.

1. Locate the height information for your favorite team. It will be published in your newspaper; you might also find it in a basketball magazine or almanac.

2. Find the average height for your team. *(You might even want to figure out the average height for the starting five players and then for the entire team.)* Then find the average height for all of the teams in your league.

3. Who are the short teams and who are the tall teams in your league? Who wins the most games? The tall teams or the short teams? Who scores the most points, taller or shorter players? Why?

4. Has the three-point rule helped make shorter players more important in basketball?

From *Basketball Math: Slam-Dunk Activities and Projects for Grades 4–8* published by GoodYearBooks. Copyright © 1995 Jack A. Coffland and David A. Coffland.

Being defensive

As in most every sport, the basketball team that plays better defense is the team that is more likely to win. Scoring may be spectacular, but defense is what wins the game. Here are the four major defensive statistics in basketball that show how the defensive team is doing.

Defensive Rebounding: One of the most important aspects of playing defense is making certain that your opponent only gets one shot at the basket. If the opposing team misses, your team must rebound to prevent second-chance points.

Steals: If one of your players can steal the ball from an opposing player, then he or she can't score because you have the ball.

Blocked Shots: Again, if one of your players can block the opponent's shot, then the ball can't go in the basket and the opponent can't score.

Turnovers: If you can steal the ball, intercept a pass, or force the other team to lose the ball out of bounds, you have again prevented the opposing team from scoring.

Keep defensive statistics on your favorite team for a game or for a season. Or, compare two teams. Which one has the better defensive statistics? If you're comparing two teams that are actually playing one another, there is an excellent chance that the one with the better defensive statistics is the winning team.

Point differential

Point differential is a statistic used to rate the overall success of basketball teams. Some teams like to play up tempo, fast break basketball with lots of scoring. Other teams like to slow the tempo of a game and concentrate on defense. Since teams use different philosophies, studying offensive or defensive statistics alone cannot tell you everything about a team's performance.

Point differential is found by subtracting the average number of the opponent's points from your team's average number of points. Chicago's +6.3, for example, means that the Bulls scored an average of 6.3 more points than their opponents throughout the season. Use the chart to answer the following questions.

1992-93

	Average points scored	Average points allowed	Point differential
Chicago	105.2	98.9	+6.3
Phoenix	113.4	106.7	
Charlotte		110.4	+0.3
L.A. Clippers	107.1		-0.3
New York	101.6	95.4	
Dallas	99.3	114.5	
Seattle	108.5	101.3	

1. What was the point differential for Phoenix?

_____

2. Charlotte's point differential was -0.3. What was the team's average number of points scored per game?

_____

3. The Clippers scored an average of 107.1 points per game and had a positive point differential of 0.3. Did they average more or fewer points than their opponents? How many points did their average opponent score? Fill in the blanks on the above chart and use the completed table to answer the questions below.

_____

From *Basketball Math: Slam-Dunk Activities and Projects for Grades 4–8* published by GoodYearBooks. Copyright © 1995 Jack A. Coffland and David A. Coffland.

4. Four of the teams listed in the chart advanced to the conference finals in the 1993 play-offs. Judging from the point differential statistic, which four teams would you guess made it to the finals?

_____

_____

_____

_____

5. Which of the listed teams would you pick as most likely to have missed the play-offs entirely?

_____

_____

_____

_____

6. The Clippers had a point differential of +0.3 and finished the regular season with exactly the same number of wins and losses, 41 of each. Charlotte had a point differential of -0.3 yet finished the season at 44–38. What could account for a Hornets' winning record but negative point differential?

_____

_____

_____

7. The four teams with the highest point differential in the chart all finished among the top five teams in the league in this category. See if you can find out which team that is not listed in the chart also finished in the top five in point differential.

_____

_____

8. Calculate the point differential for your favorite team for one week or, better yet, for one month.

_____

_____

Who's my nemesis?

Some teams seem to play particularly well against other teams. From 1991 to 1993, for example, the Chicago Bulls won three straight championships but had identical 1–5 records against San Antonio and Houston. Chicago never faced those teams in the play-offs, but if the regular season records were any indication, they might have had trouble.

In the 1993–94 regular season, Seattle had the best record in the NBA but was only 2–2 against Denver. In the same year, Utah went 5–0 against San Antonio even though the Spurs had a better record overall. In both cases, the team with the better record lost to the underdog during the playoffs.

Keep track of your favorite team's records against the rest of the league. If you record the results of each night's game on a chart, by play-off time you will know the results of the season series between your team and any other team in the league.

From *Basketball Math: Slam-Dunk Activities and Projects for Grades 4–8* published by GoodYearBooks. Copyright © 1995 Jack A. Coffland and David A. Coffland.

Can you play defense?

Sometimes a basketball player will get a reputation for scoring a lot of points but not playing any defense. On a good night, such a player might score 28 points, while the man that he guards scores only 15. The coach will look at the box score the next day and be pleased that the player scored +13. On a bad day, the same player might score 20 points but give up 35 points. When the coach sees that the player allowed 15 more points than he scored, the player might see more time on the bench.

Before a game, choose a player who has a reputation for scoring a lot of points. Keep track of how many points that player scores. Also keep track of the point total for any player he guards. At the end of the game, decide whether the player works well at both ends of the court or is primarily a scorer.

You might also look to see which player the high scorer is guarding. Is it the other team's leading scorer? Sometimes a coach will try to "hide" a weak defender by having him cover a player who doesn't shoot the ball very often. If the low scorer has a big night, you will know that the high scorer is mostly an offensive player with "no D."

When are you "above average"?

It seems to make sense that a basketball star would have his or her best games against weaker competition. Some players, however, seem to do better against the best teams and the best players. This type of player is called a "big game player."

One way to see whether a given player is a big game player is to compare that player's statistics in the important games of the year to his or her yearly averages. For example, if Shaquille O'Neal is averaging 30 points per game during the season, see how he does against another star player. If Orlando plays New York, Shaq must face Patrick Ewing, a superstar in his own right. Keep track of the points, rebounds, and blocks each of the two big men get. By comparing these numbers against the season averages, you can see whether one of the players rises to the occasion of the big game. Don't fall into the trap of generalizing from one game, however. Try to get records over several games to see who does best in the long run.

Keep a chart of your favorite player's statistics in games in which he or she plays against other big-name stars. If you find the average of these games and compare it to the seasonal average, you will get a good idea of how that player handles first-rate competition.

Backs against the wall

The NBA play-offs are a pressure cooker of excitement and
tension. Coaches and teams worry about such things as home
court advantage and adjustments made by the opposing team.
Many teams go so far as to foul rather than allow an easy basket.
The emotion can reach fever pitch.

When a play-off team is one game from elimination, it is said
to have its back against the wall. That team will play as hard as it
can since one loss will finish its season. Sometimes both teams
are one loss from elimination. This only happens in the fifth game
of a best-of-five series or the seventh game of a best-of-seven
series. During these deciding games, the pressure goes through
the roof. Watch a "back against the wall" game and see who plays
well and who does not, who scores a lot of points and who does
not. In other words, see who plays well with their "back against
the wall."

In the playoffs, wait for a deciding play-off game—one in
which the winner advances and the loser goes home—to occur.
After the game, look at the statistics for each player. Usually in a
big game, one or two players will make big plays at the end of
the game, while several others may have carried the team in the
early or middle stages. These players are generally the unsung
heroes unless they make some big plays late in the game. See if
you can identify an unsung hero who plays best when his team
has its back against the wall.

Charting the play-offs

Play-off chart

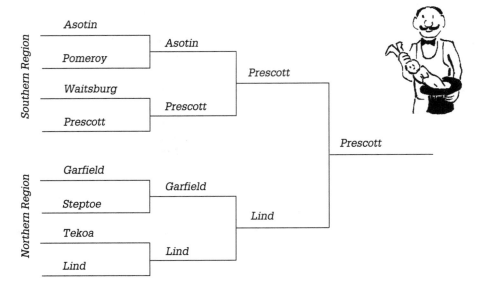

One of the things that makes basketball exciting are the play-offs. College basketball has "March Madness," where both men and women's teams are selected to play for the national championships. The NBA has an elaborate play-off system to determine its league champion. Even high schools in most states take part in play-offs to crown a state champion.

A sample play-off chart appears above. It records the eight high-school teams that started in the play-offs, located in two different brackets. Of the starting eight teams, four advanced to the second round because they won those first games. Of the four teams playing in the semi-final games, two advanced to the championship game, and of those two teams, only one wins the championship. You can see here that the Prescott Tigers have won our mythical championship.

You will find the play-off charts in your local newspaper each Spring when the college play-offs begin. Sixty-four teams are selected; 16 teams are assigned to each region. Cut out this beginning chart and record all of the winners. Or, if you prefer, make a chart for your own high school team as it moves through the state championships. Alternatively, you might make a chart showing the NBA play-offs. Fashion your handmade charts after the one pictured above.

Answer key

Answers vary in activities for which answers are not provided below.

College newspaper polls
1. 184 points
2. 1,785 points
3. 234 points
4. 25 points
Challenge: 18th

The post-season party
1. 40 games
2. 24 games
3. 4 games
4. 7 series
5. 49 games
6. 28 games
7. a. 89 games
   b. 52 games

March madness
1. 32 games
2. a. 8 games
   b. 16 teams
3. 6 rounds
Challenge problem: 9

Women's unbeaten teams
1. 2,853 points
2. 26.7 points points per game
3. 141.1 points per game
4. 34.2 field goals per game

Men's unbeaten teams
1. 323 games
2. 8 games
3. 120 wins
4. a. answer varies by year
   b. answer varies by year

The Warriors, state champs
1. a. 274 points
   b. 208 points
2. a. 68.5 points per game
   b. 52 points per game
3. 24, 6, 28, and 8 points, respectively
4. 16.5 points per game

Women's scoring champions
1. 33.0 points per game
2. 31.0 points per game
3. 907 points
4. 35 games
Challenge problem: Since all 3 players played in a different number of games, each average will need to be estimated separately. Miller's average of 29.4 points per game is highest.

The "Big O"
1. 1,052 field goals
2. 2,973 points
3. 869 free throws
Challenge problem: He averaged 33.8 points per game. They did not play the same number of games each season.

"Pistol" Pete
1. 1,387 field goals
2. 3,667 points
3. 893 free throws
Challenge problem: Answers will vary. Examples: Field goal percentage, shots per game, turnovers, etc.

Point guards
1. 2.25:1
2. 12 turnovers
3. 60 assists
4. 1.6:1
5. Efrain, who had the most assists and turnovers, started.

Women's field goal percentage leaders

Varbanova	200 field goals
Knowles	204 field goal attempts
Blocker	65.0%
Henderson	211 field goals
Vaughn	421 field goal attempts
Steward	64.3%

Comparing field goal percentages

1. 388 times
2. 776 points
3. 149 times
4. 298 points

Challenge problem: Player A's team made .9 points every time she shot the ball. Player B's team made 1.3 points for every time she shot the ball.

UCLA's string of championships

1. 13 years
2. 10 first-place finishes
3. 2 third-place finishes
4. 1 time
5. 84.6 points per game
6. 71.2 points per game
7. 13.4 points per game

Duke's shorter string of championships

1. 7 years
2. 2 first-place finishes
3. 2 second-place finishes
4. 2 times
5. 1 time
6. 71.25 points per game

NCAA women's championship results

1. a. 71 points per game
   b. 57 points per game
   c. 14 points per game
2. Southern Cal
   a. 70.5 points per game
   b. 64 points per game
   c. 6.5 points per game
   Stanford
   a. 83 points per game
   b. 71.5 points per game
   c. 11.5 points per game
   Louisiana Tech
   a. 64 points per game

b. 58 points per game
c. 6 points per game
3. 8.3 points per game
4. Old Dominion, Texas, and Texas Tech

Sheryl Swoopes, 1993 women's player of the year

1. 50.9%
2. 61 free throws
3. 9.6 rebounds per game
4. 35.4 points per game
Challenge problem: She made 8 three-point shots.

Hiding the three-point shots

Bauman	0
Swoopes	4
Pollard	0
Bascom	5
Cate	2
Swoopes	1

Mom's challenge problems

1. 15 points
2. a. 14 field goals
   b. 7 free throws
3. 70 points

Free-throw streaks I

1. 95.8%
2. a. 137 attempted
   b. 128 made
3. 93.4%
Challenge problem: You do not, because the number of shots taken for each percentage are different.

Free-throw streaks II

1. a. 305
   289
2. a. 94.8%
3. a. 90.7%
   b. 88.6%
4. Yes, Mark Price did, 94.8 to 93.7.

Hot shots

1. Anji does, with 16.1 points.
2. Anji has.
3. No, she will not.
4. 16.25 points
5. 24 points

From Basketball Math: Slam-Dunk Activities and Projects for Grades 4–8 published by GoodYearBooks. Copyright © 1995 Jack A. Coffland and David A. Coffland.

Shooting for the perimeter

1. 288 feet
2. 50 feet

Challenge problems: Perimeter = 68.8 feet,
   circumference = 37.7 feet

Covering the area

1. a. 228 square feet
   b. 456 square feet
2. 113.1 square feet
3. a. 56.6 square feet
   b. 113.1 square feet
4. 4,700 square feet

Covering the garden

1. 100 feet by 60 feet
2. 6,000 square feet
3. 16 square feet
4. 375 pieces

Going the distance

1. 56 feet
2. 6 feet
3. 22 feet
4. 119 feet
5. baseline to baseline

Shot blockers

1. 238 points
2. 234 points
3. 5.6 shots per game
4. 137 shots

Wanted for stealing

1. a. 42 points
   b. 28 points
   c. 16 points
2. 168 points

Challenge: Yes. She averages 6 steals per game, so
   she must have prevented at least 3 points.

Home-court advantage

1. +15   -1
   +17   -3
   +15   -25
   +15   -17
   -19   -25
   +33   +5
   +21   -5
   +25   +3
   -11   -27
2. a. Seattle
   b. +25 games
3. a. Minnesota
   b. -19 games
4. a. New York
   b. +5 games
5. a. Washington
   b. -27 games
6. Answers may vary.
7. +3 games

Son of home-court advantage

1. 48   34
   48   34
   36   46
   40   42
   19   63
   60   22
   49   33
   55   27
   22   60
2. +14
   +14
   -10
   -2
   -44
   +38
   +16
   +28
   -38
3. a. New York
   b. Minnesota
4. +12
5. winning, at +4
6. .500 or +0
7. Utah W47 L35
   New Jersey W43 L39
   Orlando W41 L41
8. Utah W28 L13

Amazing championship stories

1. 207 points
2. 125 points

Three famous college shot blockers
1. 308 shots
2. 5.75 shots
3. 104 shots

Challenge problem: It would be impossible to have "record performances" over every game in a season.

Senator Bradley's records
1. 24 years
2. 46 attempts

Challenge problem: There might be many players who made 1 free throw and had only 1 attempt. This would be a "cheap" record.

The long and the short of it
1. Bowie, Divac, Edwards, Campbell, and Harvey
2. 421 inches
3. 372 inches
4. 12 inches
5. 218.6 pounds
6. 263 pounds to 170 or 93 pounds.
7. 1,230 pounds and 950 pounds
8. No, it is not.
9. 215.8 pounds

Running lines
1. 470 feet
2. 2,350 feet
3. 4,700 feet
4. 423,000=80.1 miles

The "Beast of the East"
1. a. 8 teams
   b. 5 teams
2. 11 years
3. a. 80%
   b. 50%

Foul play I
1. 34.9 fouls per games
2. 9.7 fouls per games
3. 25.2 fouls per games
4. 28.4 fouls per games
5. 11 fouls per games
6. 17.4 fouls per games

Foul play II
1. 5 games
2. 1 foul
3. 2 times

Challenge problem: No, since 18 (6 fouls times 3 games) is the maximum number of fouls possible.

Growing bigger
1. 2,598.8 people
2. by 266,516 people
3. 821.8 people
4. 97,403 people

Tricky questions
1. 11
2. a. 12
   b. 1995
3. Miami, FL
4. New Mexico State and Utah State
5. a. West Virginia
   b. Arizona State and Arizona
   Note: These answers may change as teams change conference.

Division by I, II, and III
1. a. 248 points
   b. 188 points
   c. 436 points
2. I-66, II-90, III-62, combined = 72.7
3. 1,256 points

On the glass
1. 28 rebounds per game
2. 5 rebounds per game

Challenge problem: Yes, Russell had 13 more rebounds than MacAdoo and Malone combined. This makes it possible for him to have both records.

Chairman of the boards
1. a. 160 rebounds
   b. 36 rebounds
   c. 62 rebounds
   d. 62 rebounds
2. 124 rebounds
3. 98 rebounds

Challenge problem: 19 boards

From Basketball Math: Slam-Dunk Activities and Projects for Grades 4-8 published by GoodYearBooks. Copyright © 1995 Jack A. Coffland and David A. Coffland.

Where's the offense?

1. 11 points
2. 15 free throws
3. 4 field goals
4. 15 points
5. 7 shots
6. 5 points
7. Pistons 3, Lakers 1
8. No, they did not.
   .8 points per minute
9. 82 points

Where's the defense?

1. No, they did not.
2. Yes, they did
3. Denver 49, Detroit 51
4. 140 field goals
5. Denver 47, Detroit 37
6. 63 minutes
7. 2 hours 8 minutes
8. Yes, they did.
   5.87 points per minute
9. 7 points

Wilt's big night

1. a. 41 points
   b. 59 points
2. 13 points
3. 69 points
4. 28 points

Defending the big guy

1. 93
2. Yes, they did.
   103 points
3. 64 points

Double-doubles

Ethan
   Points 15, Rebounds 10,
   Assists 6, Blocks 4, Steals 2
1. a. Yes.
   b. Points and rebounds
Angela
   Points 6, Rebounds 9
   Assists 11, Blocks 1, Steals 11
2. a. Yes.
   b. assists and steals
Challenge problem: Ethan–Center, Angela–Guard

Triple-doubles

Gracie
   Points 29. Rebounds 16
   Assists 14, Blocks 7, Steals 8
Cory
   Points 32, Rebounds 21
   Assists 9, Blocks 9, Steals 11
1. Yes, both players had a triple-double.
   Gracie—Points, rebounds, assists
   Cory—Points, rebounds, steals
2. No. Yes.
3. 46 points
Challenge problem: Yes, he did.

Taking attendance

1. 40,529 fans
2. 2,541,303 fans
3. 12,888 fans
Challenge problem: Answers will vary. Example:
   Many people all over the country wanted to see
   Orlando star Shaquille O'Neal.

Keeping time

1. Chamberlain averaged more than 48 minutes per game, which is remarkable when one considers that 48 minutes is the length of a regular NBA game. Many of his games went into overtime.
2. 5 overtimes
3. 39.89 days
4. Just over 11 seasons
Challenge problem: When Bellamy was traded, his original team had played 6 more games than his new team.

NBA trivia

1. No, the Toronto Huskies played in 1946 and tied the Boston Celtics for last place in the Eastern Division.
2. the Sacramento Kings
3. a. 5 teams
   b. Golden State, in 1975
   c. L.A. Lakers, in 1972, 80, 82, 85, 87, 88
      (and as the Minneapolis Lakers, in 1949, 50, 52, 53)
   d. Portland, in 1977
   e. Sacramento, in 1951 (as the Rochester Royals)
   f. Seattle, in 1979
4. L.A. Lakers, 1971–72, 69–13

5. a. Chicago Packers, 1961–62
   b. Chicago Zephyrs, 1962–63
   c. Baltimore Bullets, 1963–64

Snack break

1. Seniors	$135.50
Juniors	$106.50
Sophomores	$63.00
Freshmen	$24.00

2. $329.00

The pep band blues

1. 187 members
2. $33.75
3. 18 sheets

Challenge problem: Kim has played 1,428 songs.
   Yes, 42 times.

Women's leading shooters

1. a. 951 points

b. Halligan	927
Jones	927
Davis	837
Savage	819

2. 2.48 three-pointers
3. Yes, there are three.
   Halligan—2.69
   Jones—2.51
   Savage—2.97

Challenge problem: Yes. Wendy Davis took almost
   the same number of shots as Middleton, but made
   many fewer. Kathy made the same number of
   shots as Julie, but played fewer games.

Accuracy counts

1. Yes, Julie took as many shots, but made fewer; her percentage will be lower.

2. Middleton	44.5%
Halligan	45.4%
Jones	43.4%
Davis	43.9%
Savage	38.6%

3. 1 Halligan
   2 Middleton
   3 Davis
   4 Jones
   5 Savage